Presented To:

_____

From:

_____

Date:

_____

PREVENTING THE MISCARRIAGE OF
DESTINY

PREVENTING THE MISCARRIAGE OF
DESTINY

STRATEGIC STEPS FOR FULFILLING YOUR GOD-GIVEN CALL

DR. GLEN A. STAPLES

DESTINY IMAGE® PUBLISHERS, INC.

P.O. Box 310, Shippensburg, PA 17257-0310

"Promoting Inspired Lives."

This book and all other Destiny Image, Revival Press, MercyPlace, Fresh Bread, Destiny Image Fiction, and Treasure House books are available at Christian bookstores and distributors worldwide.

For a U.S. bookstore nearest you, call 1-800-722-6774.

For more information on foreign distributors, call 717-532-3040.

Reach us on the Internet: www.destinyimage.com.

ISBN 13 TP: 978-0-7684-0292-6

ISBN 13 Ebook: 978-0-7684-8797-8

ISBN 13 Hardcover: 978-0-7684-4218-2

For Worldwide Distribution, Printed in the U.S.A.

2 3 4 5 6 7 8 / 16 15 14 13 12

DEDICATION

I dedicate this book to my parents, Louise and Walter Staples, the two people who were destined to be together, bring me forth, and raise me to become the man I am today. I am eternally grateful for everything they have done—for their encouragement, their correction, and most of all their display of faith.

They were the ones who showed me how to believe God, how to call upon His name, and how to trust Him. Their unique ability to bring God beyond the Sunday school lesson and beyond the Sunday service filled our house with God's reality and power. Whenever we needed something, my parents would pray and teach us that, "God will do this for us. Things will get better. Things will happen." And not only did they show us how to pray, but they also showed us how to speak as if it had already happened.

I am so proud of my father, who was an anointed preacher and a gifted prayer warrior. When he prayed, it was as if Jesus was standing right beside him. Oftentimes, the Spirit of the Lord would fall so strongly that sinners, including myself, were instantly convicted. It was wonderful to see the gifts of God work through him. I am so thankful for those experiences.

I am equally proud of my mother, who was also a gifted preacher, and who had an amazing way of speaking directly to a person's inner being. She would touch someone on the arm, look deep into the person's eyes, and make sure she had his or her full attention before saying something so powerfully simple and true that it would shoot right to the pit of the person's stomach and run all the way down to his or her toes.

I appreciate how my parents always treated me with love and respect. Even when I was in the world, they continued to treat me the way they always had. They never lectured or criticized. They just applied prayer, love, and wisdom to the situation and trusted that God would have His way—and that I would not miscarry my destiny.

I remember, on a few occasions, as I got ready to leave their home in West Virginia and return to Detroit, my mother would touch my arm, look me dead in the eye, and say, "You can't continue to live like this. You've got to give your heart to God." My father, on the other hand, would just pray or give me one of his looks that spoke volumes. Her words and his looks would often accompany me on my way back to the city. I am so thankful that they never gave up on me, loved me through it all, and continually prayed that I would fulfill the plans God had for me.

I thank God for giving me such amazing parents who raised me up with the unconditional love, abounding hope, and rock-solid faith that allowed me to birth great things.

ACKNOWLEDGMENTS

I gratefully acknowledge the many wonderful people who contributed to the writing of this book. Their generous support, encouragement, time, and dedication are truly appreciated.

First, I thank my children—Glen, Lamar, Jamie, Rodney, and Micah—for their love, their support, and their patience with me as a father.

I also thank my late wife, Martha, who has gone on to be with the Lord. She was a great inspiration to me in developing my walk with Christ and teaching me about being obedient to God. For that I am forever grateful.

Many thanks to all of my siblings, including those who have gone on to be with the Lord. Your prayers and support throughout the years have helped carry me ever onward and upward. In particular, I offer a special thanks to my sister, Johnnie Mae, who smiles down from Heaven. You always saw the best in me, believed in me, encouraged me, and trusted that I would walk into my God-ordained destiny. Long before my ordination to preach the gospel, even before I earned my first bachelor's degree, your faith led you to buy my first clergy robe, adorned with three doctoral bars. I remember how astonished I was as I questioned, "What are you doing? I can't do this. I'm just in school. I don't even have my bachelor's degree, let alone a doctorate." Your response took all of the argument out of me when you looked me in the eye and said with kindness and surety, "But you will." Thank you, Johnnie, for depositing such seeds of greatness and hope into my spiritual womb.

To my church family at the Temple of Praise in Washington, D.C., and Atlanta, Georgia, as well as the covenant churches within the Temple of Praise International Fellowship of Churches. I cherish your prayers, love, and service. I am so blessed to be your pastor. Watching you praise, worship, and grow in the Lord deeply touches my heart.

I am also grateful for each of the wonderful Spirit-filled, faithful believers who tirelessly labored with me on this manuscript. Thank you for allowing the Lord to use your time and talents. May God richly bless your selfless efforts.

Finally, I acknowledge my spiritual father, pastor, advocate, and dear friend Bishop T.D. Jakes. Your love, leadership, vision, and faithfulness have nurtured, sustained, and inspired me toward victory. Words cannot adequately express my enduring gratitude to our heavenly Father for blessing me with such an extraordinary obstetrician. To God be the glory!

ENDORSEMENT

In this latest book, Bishop Glen A. Staples unravels the perplexities that we often encounter in the conceiving, the developing, and ultimately the birthing of our God-given destiny. He brilliantly captures the trimesters that we must all live through and survive in order to actually embrace outwardly what our faith heretofore has embraced inwardly. As a prototype, he mirrors the process that a woman faces as she conceives and gives birth to a child. From the misery of morning sickness to stretch marks—conception changes everything! I believe this profound and thought-evoking read will serve as a catalyst to empower you to prepare for, protect, pray over, and ultimately push out the precious cargo called purpose that you have been carrying since before the world began. Just know that extreme pressure is only a sign that labor has begun; and we are well on our way to seeing with our eyes what we have already been seeing in our spirits! *Preventing the Miscarriage of Destiny* is not for the faint of heart; it's for those who dare to believe that "if I can dream it, I can deliver it!"

PASTOR SHERYL BRADY
Pastor, Lecturer, Recording Artist
Dallas, Texas

CONTENTS

FOREWORD

By Bishop T.D. Jakes

The wet, freezing arctic winds slicing through leafless trees formed icicles hanging like stalactites from drooping branches that surrounded the turnpike I traveled to get to the small, wood-framed church. Down a set of steps, I happened into a small room filled with joyous people whose clamorous praise conveyed their appreciation for God's grace and mercy.

When I first met Glen A. Staples, I was a twenty-something young man sporting a mass of glistening Jheri curls cascading down toward my shoulders in chemically induced ringlets. He was a young man himself whose passion for God made him a favorite among a wide variety of churches.

Glen hailed from a family known throughout the region for its pedigree of pulpiteers whose legendary style of preaching transcended barriers of denomination and race. He came from a long line of preaching-teaching giants who formed a dynasty in its own right. Still few would've imagined that Glen's journey would take him far past the storefronts of the day to the hallowed halls of universities and make its way with the gallantry of doves' wings to the status and influence that he now holds.

Today, his church, the Temple of Praise, is just that—a temple of praise and adoration to God whose worship style is unlike any other that I have ever seen or experienced in my travels throughout the world. Those who would peer through the windows into his life now would see some of the most prestigious people in Washington, D.C., looking to this man for spiritual guidance. From political giants to community activists, they come in hopes of gleaning his wisdom and approval.

Many would say he has it made. After all, he's been an invited guest at the White House; he has headed a powerhouse ministry that shut down crack houses in Southeast D.C. But before you jump to conclusions and think that his road to destiny was a clean swoop down a straight highway to a brilliant legacy, please know that Dr. Glen A. Staples has met many a rugged road as he moved toward his ultimate purpose.

Strewn along the winding path behind him is the residue of many storms that could've dissuaded a lesser man. Yet in spite of a pathway littered with tragedy, mayhem, and personal loss, he managed to steer past the cataclysmic destruction to remain relevant in the twenty-first century.

His matriculation through the hallowed halls of academia to earn two doctorate degrees is commendable for a rural boy from the foothills of the Appalachian Mountains. It is impressive, but it pales in comparison to his inner will and tenacious fortitude. It is that which we laud the loudest.

What causes him to stand head and shoulders above his peers is his unique way of absorbing unimaginable losses and catastrophic calamities like the untimely loss of his lovely wife, which left him to pastor and parent alone, and the premature demise of his siblings. I happened to witness the final departure of his sainted mother and observed him selflessly ministering to others while he silently bled himself.

But this work is far more significant than a chronicle of crises. It is a testament that the hemorrhaging of his own heart was powerless to provoke a miscarriage of his purpose. His precision as a leader has become the catalyst that earned him authority as a writer.

And because he continued to lead while bleeding, providing only a tourniquet for his own soul while dragging thousands out of the storm-tossed debris without any regard for his own pain, he has become a hero to many—though he is far too modest to acknowledge this fact.

I was pleased when I learned that he had finally decided to put pen to paper and invite us to imbibe of the bittersweet nectar of his agonizing journey and to offer it with the pure honey that is reserved for those who, like Jonathan in the Scriptures, progressed under excruciating pressure and ate for the re-fortification of their strength.

There are many who write books, but Dr. Staples' wisdom is far deeper than a scintillating sermon punctuated with salacious statistics. His voice echoes from the cavern of his soul, accentuated by his many varied experiences with dreams nursed by the perfected food warmed through the furnace of afflictions and served with a keen intellect and a sharp wit.

I can only hope that you have an appetite that is commensurate with his ability to feed that which is within you. This book was written to those who sense that they have something inside so significant that they cannot allow what is behind to deter what lies ahead.

As young men we often preached back to back in midnight youth services and camp meetings; today as elder statesmen we have continued to survive the torrential winds that yet assail us to bring a message of hope while handing a compass to the next generation who are still striving toward their aspirations.

Whether that road leads to a pulpit or a palace, business suite or corner office, pastors, entrepreneurs, and executive leaders alike will find this work transformational as they navigate life's highways, avoiding the potholes and staying on course toward destiny.

With baited breath and a sense of childhood anticipation, I encourage you to take the time to unfold this road map, the GPS system that has been compiled for those who dare to dream beyond their means and who desire to escape the mediocrity of normalcy in hopes of something beyond the status quo.

Just know that as you read each line in *Preventing the Miscarriage of Destiny* there is a flashing yellow light designed to warn you of what lies ahead and, more importantly, what needs to be flared and what needs to be flogged in order to reach your destiny and to bring to full term the seed of greatness that lies within each individual.

There is no need to have a miscarriage of destiny when what is inside you is so much greater than the obstacles around.

My friend, don't be afraid of the noisome pestilence around you, nor the gawking stares of the naysayers that pierce the darkness behind you. When all is said and done, you have the power within you to maintain your focus and keep moving!

I am excited for you to break the seal and enter the inner sanctum of Dr. Glen A. Staples' deepest thoughts and strengthen your womb of promise. Enjoy each step as he opens the road and guides you like a Sherpa past the accidents and injuries into a purpose greater than the storms you now face would tell you about your future.

Where you are going is far more significant than where you have been. Take a moment, if you are willing, and survey the topography of what lies ahead. To be forewarned is to be forearmed.

Ladies and gentlemen, I commend you to God and the wise tutelage of a sage voice of wisdom and will. As his pastor, I am proud to introduce to some and present to others your tour guide to destiny, Dr. Glen A. Staples.

BISHOP T.D. JAKES
Senior Pastor
The Potter's House of Dallas, Inc.

INTRODUCTION

Have you ever wondered why some people succeed in accomplishing all that God has called them to do, while others continually fall short? Is it possible that those who do not reach their God-ordained destiny simply misinterpret or mishandle the trials and tribulations in their lives? Could it be that they misunderstand the role of pain and interpret it as failure, rather than part of the process of success?

I ask again, but more personally, have you ever wondered why others seem to achieve their full potential in God while, often, you seem to miss the mark? If your answer is yes, prayerfully reading this book will shed light on your current situation, helping you obtain the foreordained goals and purposes for your life and enabling you to produce greater results in God, for His Kingdom.

Throughout the pages of this book, we will consider the *spiritual* birthing process in light of what we know about the *physical* birthing process. I have learned that throughout our lives the Lord orchestrates this birthing process in order to bring us to the place where we can deliver the great things He has deposited inside us. I believe, if we reflect on the process of physical conception and the birthing of a child, we can identify important insights about the way we ought to spiritually conceive and birth our destiny.

I pray that you will understand and embrace your seasons of preparation and that you will use the tools provided in this analogy to evaluate, nurture, and protect the promise that is growing inside you. I assure you—preventing the failure, annihilation, and destruction of God's preordained promises *is* possible.

Join me on this spiritual journey to prevent the miscarriage of destiny!

> *May you always be filled with the fruit of your salvation—the righteous character produced in your life by Jesus Christ—for this will bring much glory and praise to God* (Philippians 1:11 NLT).

CHAPTER I

IT STARTS WITH A SEED

Now the parable is this: The seed is the
word of God (Luke 8:11 NKJV).

In the beginning was the Word, and the Word was
with God, and the Word was God (John 1:1 NKJV).

In the beginning, nothing existed. In the beginning, God created everything. In fact, God spoke, and His Word was the seed that started all of creation. Creation started with just a seed; human life starts with a seed; even our own destiny begins with a seed.

I have come to the conclusion that the physical process of having a baby, from conception to delivery, is comparable to the spiritual process of giving birth to destiny. We know that the seed of a man is released during an intimate act. When the seed fertilizes an egg, a life is generated and is, subsequently, implanted in the womb of a woman.

During conception, the sperm of a man carries genetic instructions (referred to as DNA) into the egg of a woman, which also contains an abundance of genetic information. The result of this fragile fusing is the miraculous development of a brand-new human life. So it is with the conception of destiny.

In order for *spiritual* pregnancy to occur, seed must be released before it can bind with what God has already placed inside us. Once fertilization occurs, what God has established can be firmly attached inside our spiritual wombs. We are now poised to give birth to destiny, vision, and purpose.

Indeed, the word "sperm" is derived from the Greek word *sperma,* which means seed. Once seed is deposited, received by the egg, and embedded in our hearts and souls, it grows and produces marvelous results in our lives and in the lives of the people who encounter the fruit of our spiritual womb. However, we must learn how to conceive first, and then we must discover our responsibility to nurture and protect this fertilized egg from harm and expulsion. We must protect the embryo of destiny in its earliest stage of development so that vision can properly mature and purpose can begin to take shape.

WHAT IS SEED? FROM WHERE DOES IT COME?

As we begin reviewing the process of giving birth to destiny, let us take a spiritual look at the concept of seed. Spiritual seed comes in many forms, including things we hear, see, feel, and experience. Seed can be direct (obvious) behaviors and words (spoken or withheld), or seeds can be indirect (subtle) in the form of innuendos, motifs, and body language. Seed can often be identified as recurring patterns or as defining moments that connect to our "self." Once the seed attaches to the core of our being, it begins to fill the space where vision and purpose will either thrive or die.

> **Even if you are not aware of a deposit,
> seeds are released that shape and
> give substance to your life.**

People are often the primary depositors of the various kinds of seeds that are sown into our lives. For example, during our intimate conversations and relationships with friends and family, the exchange of information functions as seed. Even when we are not aware that the origin of something great is being deposited, seeds are released, which ultimately give shape and substance to our lives. I can recall specific examples of this occurring in my own life.

From a young age, whenever people prayed for or prophesied over me, they would mention the call on my life to preach the gospel of Jesus Christ. However, I specifically remember one particular incident when my grandmother released such a seed into my life, which really took hold in my spirit. It occurred when I was around twelve years of age, within the intimacy of our own home. That morning, my grandmother sat, reading her newspaper, on the edge of the pull-out couch where my brother and I slept. I abruptly awoke, sat up, and glanced around the room with a frightened look on my face. Sensing my fear, my grandmother asked, "What's wrong, son? Did you have a bad dream?"

Immediately I replied, "Grandma, I think I just dreamed about hell!" Then, with great emotion, I began to tell her what I saw. I told her that there were people running and screaming, and there was fire everywhere, but the fire wasn't affecting me. I was just standing there, and the people were running right past me. They were screaming and hollering—and were on fire. I was terrified. I wanted to help them, but I couldn't because they were already enflamed. When I tried to speak, they couldn't hear me. I could only observe their suffering. Some of them were running. Some were falling down and being overtaken by the flames.

I will never forget the unbearable, overwhelming feeling of sorrow and compassion that I had for those people. It broke my heart. I wanted to help them, but I couldn't because they were already in judgment.

When I finished telling my grandmother the horrifying details of my nightmare, she gently looked at me, smiled, and said with surety, "Yeah, God's going to use you, son. He's going to use you to preach the gospel. God showed you that so you could tell others not to go to that place." Then she calmly went back to reading her newspaper like it wasn't anything.

The seed that my grandmother planted that morning confirmed what I was feeling. I was too late to help the people who were already in hell, but I wasn't too late to help the people who were on their way to hell.

The fear and shock of that nightmare, combined with the seed my grandmother planted, shook my spirit awake. Though others had previously told me I was going to be a preacher, I didn't really understand what that meant. I just kind of accepted it in a serious, childlike attitude of, "Okay. Okay." However, the intimacy of that morning with my grandmother confirmed what I felt the dream was telling me. From that moment on, I began to understand what the call on my life to preach really meant.

Though I was years from completely understanding what the Lord had created me to do, the knowledge contained within that seed was enough to carry me through to the birthing of my destiny to preach the salvation of Jesus Christ to a lost and dying world. In fact, that seed, planted nearly fifty years ago, is still bearing fruit today.

Many have experienced the deposit of a divine seed of destiny into their lives. Perhaps you have heard the story that writer and producer Tyler Perry tells about how Oprah Winfrey unknowingly set his career in motion by encouraging individuals to write down their painful experiences as a way to move beyond them. Tyler's writing, which often addresses painful or difficult subjects, typically leads from forgiveness to healing, and eventually to deliverance—not only for him, but for many people who are touched by his words and success.

As the previous examples illustrate, words can be much more than a momentary transmittal of information. The information deposited during a communication exchange may carry *seeds* that have the power to transform and save lives.

THE POWER OF SEED

During the early years of a child's life, the mind, in its rudimentary stages of development, is most impressionable. This is why some psychologists use the term "formative years" to describe this stage of an individual's life. Think, for instance, of a father who tells his daughter that she will never amount to anything. Most of us can recall children who were told this. When their perception of what was being said became their reality, the negative message functioned as seed by producing negative behaviors and destructive thought patterns!

Alternatively, consider two children playing baseball and supporting one another with cheers and words of affirmation. Their seeds of encouragement will, most likely, have a positive impact on each child's destiny! Whether good or evil, whether positive or negative, words have the ability to formulate our perception of who we are and who we will become.

> The power of a single seed,
> when planted in good ground,
> has unlimited potential!

It is important to note that a single seed can produce a single call; and from that call, one can be led in many different directions. For example, in educational and professional environments, each seed of information we receive can potentially affect our personal *and* professional development. In these settings, as we participate and progress through different sessions and subjects, the topics we grasp both inspire and transform our perceptions, values, and beliefs. As professors and instructors sow into our futures, we ultimately give birth to certifications, diplomas, degrees, professions, and careers.

Each informational seed that we receive has the potential to grow into knowledge; and, in turn, that knowledge can evolve into power. The power of a single seed, when planted in good ground, has unlimited potential!

Like a child, the more receptive we are to the various forms of seed introduced into our lives, the more likely something that has been poured into us will come out in the future. This manifestation will present itself in a variety of forms that, typically, resemble what was taken in by the receiver. Just as the seeds that are sown in academic and professional fields can lead to great accomplishments, so the seeds that are sown in personal relationships can also propel us toward greatness. For example, who knew that over the course of my spiritual journey, my grandmother's simple statement would empower me to become a teacher, counselor, coach, armorbearer, assistant pastor, pastor, entrepreneur, and now a bishop who oversees hundreds of churches around the world?

> *And he gave some, apostles; and some, prophets; and some, evangelists; and some, pastors and teachers; for the perfecting of the saints, for the work of the ministry, for the edifying of the body of Christ* (Ephesians 4:11-12).

THE ROMANCE OF SEED

Most of the time, when we contemplate physical conception, we tend to attribute the act of intimacy to an attraction between a man and a woman. Likewise, there is a powerful parallel that takes place in the spiritual realm. I am inclined to suggest that there is even a *spiritual romance* between the pulpit and the pew. When a Spirit-filled pastor and Spirit-filled people come together, with the honorable intention of getting caught up in the intimacy of holiness, a wooing or a drawing occurs between that Spirit-led pastor and his Spirit-following flock.

Churches, therefore, are captivating settings for the release of seed. The relationship between a preacher and his parishioner creates an opportunity for the transfer of seed into the belly of the saint, where the spiritual reproduction system resides and where the development and nourishment of destiny transpires. When an apostle, prophet, evangelist, pastor, or teacher begins to speak, the word of God comes forth as seed. As the word (seed) penetrates the saint's maturing visions, dreams, and desires, God's preordained promise is formed and attached to the fertile lining of a parishioner's spiritual womb.

Have you ever attended a church service and, after the pastor preached, you left the sanctuary on fire for the Lord? Perhaps the thunderous teaching and preaching of God's Word energized you like never before and motivated you to begin looking for an opportunity to serve in the Kingdom. Perhaps the preached word was so powerful and specific that you became inflamed with the desire to transform yourself from a pew member to a co-laborer in Christ! Well, my dear brother or sister, if you have ever encountered such a powerful experience, then you were impregnated with a word that was designed for that specific purpose in your life! The Word of God, as expounded upon and preached by the man or woman of God, revealed your destiny to you.

The Lord gives us pastors who operate as parental figures so they can pour into our lives. Not only do they impregnate us with a *rhema*[1] word of promise, they also provide us with the principles of achieving our promise. This is the effect of preaching! This is the power of the pulpit! Once the word is revealed, it can connect (fertilize) to the promise (egg) that God has placed within our spiritual wombs. Later we will discuss our responsibility to protect and nourish the fertilized egg.

Before I formed thee in the belly I knew thee; and
before thou camest forth out of the womb I sanctified
thee… (Jeremiah 1:5).

Not only do we receive seed through our daily interactions with the external world, but we also receive seed as a result of an inward personal relationship with Christ. When we pray and fast, when we mediate and wail, when we seek and petition "Abba Father," when we intentionally position ourselves at the foot of God's throne and intentionally open ourselves up to His presence, that is when God's seed of destiny is deposited into our lives. That is when we are able to hear His Holy Spirit speak to our inner being. That is when He calls us, when He directs us, when He leads us. That is when He guides us to do His good and perfect will.

When we open ourselves up to hear God's voice, He will reveal His plan. He will reveal our purpose. As we listen to His voice, purpose rises up, and His Spirit inspires us to cultivate the seed of purpose that He has sown within our spiritual wombs.

We may be tempted to create, or manage, the terms and conditions that set the birth of our destiny in motion. We may reason that, by doing so, we will reduce the factors that may lead to the premature birth, or even the miscarriage, of our destiny. However, Proverbs 14:12 warns, *"There is a way that seems right to a man, but its end is the way of death"* (NKJV). Therefore, it is essential that we remain alert to the settings where the seed of destiny is able to be released.

FOR BETTER OR WORSE—THE IMPACT OF INTIMACY

We know that with physical conception there is a measure of intimacy (a closeness or connection), which sets the stage for seed to be deposited. As already suggested in regard to spiritual conception, seed is released in a variety of (intimate) settings and is manifested in many forms, including thoughts, actions, words, and deeds. We are most aware that the possibility of receiving seed happens when we intentionally place ourselves in situations where we expect to be taught or inspired, such as in church or at school. However, we need to be more attentive to those unplanned or spontaneous interactions that set us up to receive ideas or instructions unconsciously.

For example, engaging in intimate conversation is one of the most profound, but not always obvious, acts that can create an atmosphere ripe for the release of seed. Even during intimate conversations with a stranger, such conversations can lead to attachments, which mimic certain "relationship" characteristics. This emotional openness provides the perfect opportunity for the entrance, or deposit, of information.

Scripture clearly reveals that one purpose for intimate relationships is reproduction. Genesis 4:1 states, *"Now Adam knew Eve his wife, and she conceived and bore Cain..."* (NKJV). Through their relationship, seed was deposited and a new life was created. Of course, there was a physical knowing (an intimate act that produced a child). We can safely assume that, since Eve was "bone of his bone and flesh of his flesh," Adam also had an *emotional* connection and rapport with his wife. Their emotional connection paved the way for the intimate act that resulted in the seed, the conception, and the birth of their son.

You may have heard the word "intimacy" decoded as "into me see." I first heard this wonderful insight from my spiritual father. Think about it: during intimate encounters, we allow someone to see into us. When we find ourselves involved in intimate encounters, especially through emotional conversations, there is always a release. If we are not careful, we can unknowingly leave ourselves vulnerable to the introduction of seed that produces distraction, disease, disobedience, discouragement, defeat, and ultimately death—*miscarriage.*

Intimacy suggests that a connectedness, or closeness, exists between individuals. Usually, we are not surprised when people we choose to have close relationships with (friends, spouse, etc.) affect our behavior. After all, the amount of time and energy we spend with them naturally progresses us through the various layers of intimacy. However, we are less aware of the impact individuals may have on us when they are connected to us by chance, such as siblings (who may behave in ways that are totally opposite to our own behaviors) or individuals (who attend the same place of worship).

I recall that shortly after I arrived in the District of Columbia in 1990, individuals with whom I attended church planted a negative seed of doubt concerning my purpose to preach. Thankfully, the close connection between the Lord, my wife, Martha (who has since gone home to glory), and I protected and sustained the word over my life to preach.

For the seven previous years, while in West Virginia, I was accustomed to preaching up to two and three times every Sunday. It was such a wonderful experience. Even after moving to Washington that July, I continued to receive regular invitations to preach for various pastors in the city when they went on vacation. Then, by late September, my preaching invitations suddenly stopped.

Finally in November, as the associate pastor of the 10th Street Baptist Church, an opportunity to preach in my pastor's stead arose. As my pastor prepared to go out of town, I prepared to preach with great anticipation and appreciation. Since I hadn't preached in several weeks, I fasted and prayed, "Oh, God, let me go over here and do a good job."

As my wife and I neared the church on the evening I was scheduled to preach, we noticed several members of our congregation departing in what appeared to be a hasty manner. Concerned by the looks on their faces, I rolled down my car window and asked them why they were leaving. With disgust they replied, "Someone else is preaching. We're just going to go home. We aren't going to sing."

Apparently, there was miscommunication between the two church offices. Unfortunately, no one had relayed any change of plan to *me*. In response to what I considered a personal affront, my initial thought was to immediately leave. I must admit, I was also hurt and confused. God had clearly sent me to D.C., but I couldn't help but wonder if He was playing some cruel game with me, or if I was doing something to cause this preaching drought. So, I prayed, "What are You doing, Lord? Or, what is it that I'm not doing? What is it?"

Lacking an answer and filled with indignation and doubt, I turned to my wife and said, "Let's go."

The emotions behind my words reflected the negative seed that had been sown by the brothers and sisters from our congregation. Because we were emotionally attached, through our worship and labor of our Lord, my spiritual womb was opened to the seeds they released.

Fortunately, their negative seeds were unable to penetrate the strength of my wife's character and take root in her heart. Calmly, she looked at me and stated with dignity, "You're better than that. Let's go in here and hear a word. Just because you're not preaching doesn't mean that we don't need a word. And you need one now."

Her simple message, intimately spoken, transformed my defeated and disappointed disposition. Because of the depth of our relationship and the maturity of my own character, I was able to immediately embrace the life-giving seed she released.

With that, we got out of the car, entered the sanctuary, and took seats in the rear. Eventually someone mentioned to the pastor that I was there. Though still distracted, I heard someone ask, "Is Reverend Staples here?"

To which I replied, "Yes."

"Come up and join us."

I proceeded toward the platform where the preachers were sitting, and after the preacher preached, the pastor of the church said, "We have a couple of preachers here. Let them have a word, and then we are going to dismiss."

When it was my turn to speak, I stood up and walked to the pulpit. I honestly can't recall *what* I said. I was only up there about three minutes. What I do know is that the power of the Lord so filled the place that the people erupted in praise. When I sat down, people were jumping up and hollering and screaming. The pastor looked at me and said, "Boy, God's all over you." Then he asked me a question that still brings a smile to my face, "What are you doing the first Sunday in December?"

"My schedule is open," I replied with delight. "I'm not doing anything."

My once empty calendar soon became so full that I, regretfully, had to decline several invitations. I can't *imagine* what would have happened had I not been receptive to my wife's seed of encouragement. Perhaps I could have miscarried or aborted my destiny; I don't know. However, I do know that it is crucial for us to continually grow in the knowledge of God and nurture an ability to discern when a life-giving seed is released and when a destructive seed is released.

SEEKING GOOD SEED

As we push toward our destiny, it is important that we are mindful of the fact that intimacy always provokes passion—and passion unbridled can produce sin. For this reason, we must guard who we talk with, what we talk about, and what we watch or read. We must continually seek out good seed because tainted seed sown into good ground can produce corrupt fruit.

Consider Demetrius, the talented and successful silversmith of Ephesus.[2] For financial gain, he used his gifts and his calling to produce silver idols of the goddess Diana. Demetrius clearly understood that the spread of the gospel would threaten his income. Consumed with passion for his livelihood, he persuaded the Ephesians to reject the call of Christ as preached by Paul.

Had this passionate silversmith opened his heart to the life-giving words of the gospel, he would have heard the Holy Spirit's instructions to use his God-given abilities to serve Christ. Instead, he chose to create idols. Rather than leading others toward the love of the only true and living God, Demetrius led others on a path of destruction. He could have blessed himself and others by producing much-needed items. Sadly, he willingly joined his intended blessing with a tainted seed sown by idol worshipers. Tainted seed sown into good ground can lead to death.

THE PURPOSE OF SEED

It is clear that there is an ultimate purpose for seed: *production!* In the physical, as well as in the spiritual, when seed is released, something is meant to come forth. One thing is very definite about seed—it produces its own kind. You've heard the phrase, "An apple doesn't fall far from the tree," meaning children inherit some of their parents' traits (good and bad); and perhaps you've heard, "She (or he) spit him out," meaning children inherit some of their parents' physical characteristics. Along those same lines spiritually, if negative seed connects to what is in us and is given a place to grow, it will produce negative results. Likewise, if the seed is positive, the results will be positive.

Seed is also intended to carry information (instructions) that will be used to develop and direct a new life. When a man and a woman come together, seed is released and received. The information contained in the father's sperm then joins with the information that exists in the mother's egg. We refer to this information as DNA (deoxyribonucleic acid), otherwise known as the "secret of life" or the "building blocks of life." The messages transmitted by the DNA control characteristics such as sex, coloring (hair, skin, and eyes), and blood type.

Just as the physical seed of a man contains *physical* DNA, the spiritual seed that God releases contains *spiritual* DNA. Therefore, God's seed (His word) is actually the ordained vehicle that He uses to transport us to our destiny. In fact, our heavenly Father lovingly orchestrates our lives in such a way that the seed He releases is able to join up with the spiritual DNA that He has already placed inside us. The New International Version of the Bible tells us in Psalm 139:13 that God knit us together and created our inmost being. Within the center of our innermost being, God wisely placed all of the emotions, moral sensitivity, and ability needed to navigate us on our journey and to lead us to our destinies.

Just as the prophet Jeremiah's life was set in motion before his very existence, so it is with both your natural and spiritual destinies. Before your parents existed, God knew you and pre-ordained the direction for your life. At a very young age, the Lord revealed to Jeremiah that his purpose (genetic makeup) was the prophetic office. In fact, the Hebrew name "Jeremiah" means "Yahweh hurls."[3] One can only imagine the seed that was released each time Jeremiah's name was spoken—reminding him of the call on his life and connecting him to the purpose of his destiny.

Knowing that the call to be a prophet can overwhelm and frighten a child (or an adult), God maneuvered Jeremiah into situations and circumstances that prepared, protected, and delivered his gift. It was the Lord who enabled Jeremiah to fulfill his destiny. Look at how God works! As Jeremiah was instructed to speak on God's behalf, a positive seed of encouragement was deposited into the young prophet's innermost being. At the same time that encouragement was released, another seed was released, which instructed Jeremiah to reject the negative seed of fear that had been generated by self-doubt. Jeremiah 1:4-8 reads:

> *Then the word of the LORD came unto me, saying, Before I formed thee in the belly I knew thee; and before thou camest forth out of the womb I sanc- tified thee, and I ordained thee a prophet unto the nations. Then said I, Ah, Lord GOD! behold, I cannot speak: for I am a child. But the LORD said unto me, Say not, I am a child: for thou shalt go to all that I shall send thee, and whatsoever I command thee thou shalt speak. Be not afraid of*

their faces: for I am with thee to deliver thee, saith the LORD.

Once we learn that God has woven us together and shaped us for a specific destiny, once we realize that the seed (instructions and information) serves a specific purpose, it is quite natural for us to desire that God would show us our end, even while we are at the beginning. However, if He did so, we would be tempted to take an alternative path and avoid the hard trials and tribulations, which God allows, in order to mature our inner being. Without this strengthening process, we would not be capable of carrying our promise to full term and push forth our destiny at its appointed time. Or, perhaps, we wouldn't move at all, creating a spiritual stagnation that would ultimately lead to the miscarriage of our destinies. Although seed has the potential to produce everything we require, the character and tenacity we gain as we *progress* are the very things we need to sustain us in the *process* of achieving our destinies.

As you get ready to turn this page, let me encourage you to begin preparing yourself to move closer to the delivery of your destiny. Determine to remind yourself that the information contained in the seed will keep you on track and act as a spiritual compass during trials, tribulations, and the occasional misinterpretation of your destiny. In stressful seasons, when uncertainty breeds frustration, fear, and doubt, you may ask yourself, "Where do I go from here? What should be my next step? Am I going in the right direction?" However, just remember that the spiritual DNA contained within your blessing will provide the wisdom, understanding, and strength you need to hold on tight and not let go. Hold fast to your faith as we continue on our journey and begin to focus our attention on the conditions of conception because *you* have been *chosen to receive!*

ENDNOTES

1. *Rhema* word: the voice of the Holy Spirit as it speaks to the believer at the present moment.

2. See Acts 19:24-41.

3. "Jeremiah (2)," *International Standard Bible Encyclopedia,* accessed March 30, 2012, http://www.biblestudytools.com/encyclopedias/isbe/jeremiah-2.html.

CHAPTER 2

CHOSEN TO RECEIVE

And the angel came in unto her, and said, Hail,
thou that art highly favoured, the Lord is with thee:
blessed art thou among women (Luke 1:28).

Can you imagine being Mary, the mother of Jesus, favored and chosen by God? Consider being overshadowed by the Holy Ghost and learning that buried within your womb is the seed who will save the world. What would it be like to produce in the physical world that which was conceived in the spiritual, to carry inside you a seed deposited without any physical contact?

Beloved, like Mary, you can also experience a type of Immaculate Conception! You *can* experience being overshadowed by the power of the Holy Ghost. You *can* receive a seed who will not only change your life, but will also, ultimately, impact the world!

Since we are well aware of our own imperfections, it is often difficult for us to believe we are able to manifest a destiny that is world-changing. However, God can use anybody, no matter his or her background or ability. We do not have to be perfect to be chosen by God. According to the wisdom of men, Mary, an unwed commoner from disrespected Nazareth, was not the perfect, or even most likely, candidate to conceive the word and birth the deliverance of her fellow Jews and the entire human race.

> **You do not have to be perfect to be chosen by God.**

God consistently confuses the wisdom of man by using controversial situations and choosing unlikely, complicated candidates to conceive, carry, and deliver His blessings. Even though the enemies of the Lord scheme to destroy God's chosen blessing-carriers, God turns the enemy's plans upside down so that, when success is manifested, it is obvious that all the glory belongs to the Lord. The Bible is full of the evidence proclaimed in Romans 8:28: *"...all things work together for good to them that love God, to them who are the called according to his purpose."*

Along with Mary, Moses' life also demonstrates how God receives glory by turning negative situations into positive outcomes. When the king of Egypt designed a plan to control and suppress his Hebrew slaves, his mind could not have conceived the terror that would soon plague his kingdom. Ironically, Pharaoh actually birthed his own oppression when he ordered the drowning of the newborn Hebrew sons. The monarch's scheme actually promoted a powerless condemned infant into a powerful deliverer who (with God's help) would drown an entire Egyptian army.

God spared the infant Moses when He inspired Jochebed to send her son down river in a make-shift ark. To the human mind, delivering a three-month-old infant into the hands of his executioner seems ludicrous—but to God, it made perfect sense. Before Moses saw the light of day, the Lord chose him to deliver God's beloved people from their misery. So, in a bizarre twist of events that could have only been orchestrated by the Lord, Pharaoh became Moses' adoptive grandfather, and his birth mother (yes, the one who disobeyed Pharaoh's order) became his hired nursemaid.

Hallelujah!

Our God spared a newborn slave and set him up to be raised as royalty! God knew His chosen blessing-carrier would benefit from a formal education, so He placed him under the tutelage of the most powerful contemporary ruler of that time. In my mind, Moses' training held great significance when he later faced Pharaoh and demanded he let God's people go.

According to God's design, by the time Moses reached physical maturity and learned that he was, in fact, a Hebrew, he was well on his way to being fully prepared for the conception of his destiny—to deliver the nation of Israel out of bondage and into their purpose. As the Lord began Moses' spiritual education, He opened the young man's eyes to the surrounding injustice. One day, while witnessing an Egyptian oppressor beating a Hebrew slave, Moses lost control of his emotions and murdered the oppressor. When Pharaoh heard of this, he tried to kill Moses, but Moses fled to the wilderness to avoid justice. In spite of Moses' criminal background, God chose to send the fugitive murderer back to the place of his crime so he could free the nation of Israel from

Pharaoh's bondage and deliver them into their Promised Land of milk and honey.

Throughout history, against all odds, other unlikely individuals have risen beyond their humble or chaotic circumstances in order to conceive and birth great destinies. In the fall of 2006, Alejandro Botticelli[1] gave 3-1 odds that Hillary Clinton would be elected as the 44th President of the United States. The next probable candidate for the position, John McCain, held 6-1 odds. Trailing in the polls that fall, with 10-1 odds, was an African American junior United States Senator named Barack Obama. Even with the odds stacked against this seemly unlikely candidate, he won the electoral college by a margin of 2-1.

Primarily raised by his white grandparents, Obama was, in his own words, the son of a "white as milk" American mother and a "black as pitch" Kenyan father. After his parents divorced, when Barack was just two years old, his father left his son behind and returned to Kenya. In his personal narrative, *Dreams from My Father*, Obama openly shared his early, poor choices, which started in high school and ended in college.

Torn by the chaos of oppression and self-doubt, Obama, like countless other confused individuals, used mind-altering substances to cope with his frustrations. Admitting his struggle for racial identity, he said:

> We were always playing on the white man's court...
> by the white man's rules. If the principal, or the
> coach, or a teacher...wanted to spit in your face, he
> could, because he had the power and you didn't....
> The only thing you could choose was withdrawal
> into a smaller and smaller coil of rage. And the final

irony: should you refuse this defeat and lash out at your captors…they would have a name for that too. Paranoid. Militant.[2]

Regarding his self-medication, Obama humbly admitted:

Pot had helped, and booze; maybe a little blow when you could afford it. Junkie. Pothead. That's where I'd been headed: the final, fatal role of the young would-be black man…I got high [to] push questions of who I was out of my mind.[3]

It doesn't sound like he was destined to become the future president of the United States, does it?

Other seemingly unlikely men overcame unfavorable odds to birth great destinies. College dropout Bill Gates not only co-founded and managed Microsoft, but he also became one of the world's richest and most generous philanthropists. Albert Einstein, one of the most respected scientists in history, did not speak until the age of three. His severe underachievement in elementary school led his parents to believe that he might be retarded. Renowned composer Ludwig van Beethoven created beautiful musical masterpieces such as *Symphony No. 2, op. 36 (D Major)*, *Symphony No. 3 Eroica, op. 55 (E flat Major)* and *Symphony No. 4, op. 60 (B flat Major)* after he lost his hearing. High school dropout Tyler Perry, discussed in the first chapter, grew up in a troubled home in the hardened, poverty-stricken streets of New Orleans. However, he is now a multimillion-dollar Hollywood A-lister and the first African American owner of a major film and television studio.

Several seemingly unlikely women also birthed greatness, though their personal circumstances suggested the "outcomes" of their lives should be limited. Oprah Winfrey, a black American media personality, actress, producer, literary critic, and magazine publisher, was born to unwed teen parents; she was poor while growing up in the South during the late 1960s; and she engaged in destructive behavior as a way to deal with the pain and anger caused from being a sexually abused child. It would be understandable if these circumstances limited her life chances, but, instead, she became the first African American female billionaire and owner of a television network.

Agnes Gonxhe Bojaxhiu, better known as Mother Teresa, was a mild-mannered, diminutive Albanian woman whose father died when she was about eight, sending the family into poverty. Regardless, she created a worldwide network of missions that included, by the time of her death in 1997, 4,000 members (nuns) who were established in 610 foundations in 123 countries—with more than one million volunteers caring for the poorest of the poor's physical and spiritual needs. She was awarded the Nobel Peace Prize in 1979.[4]

Helen Keller overcame deafness and blindness to become the first deaf and blind person to earn a bachelor of arts degree. During her worldwide travels, she raised funds for disabled people and various other causes. In addition, this true pioneer also became a successful lecturer, author, activist, and world leader who positively impacted millions of lives.

After she was hit with an iron weight thrown by an enraged overseer at a fleeing slave, Harriet Tubman was plagued by seizures, narcolepsy, and chronic headaches. In spite of her disabilities and the watchful eye of her master, she managed to not only birth her own freedom, but also the freedom of hundreds of enslaved African Americans. This tough, pistol-wearing conductor of the

Underground Railroad never lost a "traveler." Listed among her other accomplishments are abolitionist, humanitarian, nurse, and Union spy.[5]

Though I was born into a family of preachers and the seed that I would preach had already been deposited into me when I was called by God, I struggled to see beyond my imperfections and comprehend God's will and His ability to use me. You see, as a street-wise, drug-addicted, temper-riddled young man, I was not the most likely candidate to succeed, even in the most basic sense of being able to provide for myself or a family. When I looked in the mirror, it was even harder for me to see myself as a preacher of the gospel or a pastor. The heavy responsibility of shepherding a flock was way beyond my own comprehension.

> **Your qualifications to carry and birth a great destiny hinge on God's power and glory.**

Although you may believe that there are others more worthy of being chosen by God for a good or important work, remember that *"we are all as an unclean thing, and all our righteousnesses are as filthy rags"* (Isa. 64:6a). Your qualifications for success do not hinge on your ability or your previous accomplishments! Your qualifications to carry and birth a great destiny hinge on God's power and glory—not on your own. All you have to do is trust Him, obey Him, and submit to His good and perfect will. Remember, we are each *"fearfully and wonderfully made"* (Ps. 139:14); or as Ethel Waters, African American jazz singer, put it: "God don't make no junk."

So, relax, rejoice, and receive the destiny that resides within you. After all, it is designed to produce a life of purpose and promise.

OPEN TO RECEIVE

As discussed in Chapter 1, although we daily receive spiritual seed from a number of sources, the conditions must be right for an individual seed to enter an individual egg cell. Cells are the basic units on which the structure of life is built. In other words, cells function as the building blocks (both good and bad) of our lives. Eggs are among the largest and most visible cells in our body. From a spiritual sense, they represent the information about yourself that cannot be hidden—like when strangers saw the preacher in me before I knew I was called to preach.

During spiritual conception, when the seed fuses itself to what is already in us (our egg), the basic structure of the seed and the egg are transformed and changed. Once the seed and egg connect, they no longer function as individual entities. Now they function as one. Now they are a new creation. In other words, *old things are passed away; behold, all things are become new*" (2 Cor. 5:17b).

As in the physical realm, though the new creation has come into existence, its delivery does not happen immediately. In order for our destiny to properly develop, our newly created blessing (our fertilized egg) must first embed itself in the center of our soul, at the core of our being. However, before it can attach itself to the wall of our spiritual womb, we must be receptive to the Holy Spirit. When God chose Mary, she was open to receiving that which seemed unlikely. She was willing to reach beyond her own capacity of understanding. In order to "make it happen," she willingly surrendered her body and her life to God.

Blessed is she who has believed that the Lord would fulfill his promises to her! (Luke 1:45 TNIV)

As I see it, this is what took place in the life of Tyler Perry. Oprah Winfrey's words were the seed that fused with his gifts and experiences. After conception occurred, his pain and bondage transformed into a story of forgiveness and healing, which [in]-formed the shape and characteristics of Perry's writing and producing. Similar to other God-ordained unions, the fully developed blessing (Perry's career) became a vehicle to inspire, strengthen, and save God's people. What a miracle! Imagine…the seed that Oprah Winfrey deposited into Perry's life and that he willingly received became part of a reproductive system that perpetually produces additional seed. Destiny begets destiny.

Destiny begets destiny.

As I have already stated, God uses a variety of places and situations to release seed into our lives. Each time we enter a schoolhouse, workplace, or worship service, we are exposed to seed. Each time we open our Bibles and read the Word of God, seed is released. Each time we pray and go before the throne of God, seed is released. The "daily bread" (or "daily seed") that we seek provides the information, instruction, and order we need to progress toward our purpose. In order to connect us to our purposed destiny, God can use any setting to release His preordained seed into our spiritual wombs. Indeed, many saints who have walked with the Lord for some length of time have most likely experienced days when it appears that no matter what they are doing, saying, seeing, or hearing, the Lord is speaking.

Seasoned saints *frequently* find themselves in a place where seed is released. Their maturity causes them to be open and receptive to God as He speaks in and through them. In other words, they are ovulating and ready for conception. They are ready for destiny to be established in their spiritual wombs! My next question to you is, "Are *you* ready to receive your seed?"

God uses people who are ready, willing, and able to have their egg of destiny fertilized. In other words, God uses people who are spiritually ovulating. Consider Luke, chapter 5. Seasoned fishermen Simon, James, and John toiled all night, yet failed to catch any fish. Nevertheless, at Jesus' word, they again let down their nets, even though they were tired, it was late, and it seemed improbable that they would catch anything. Though they were physically tired, their spirits were open to instruction; they were ovulating. Their willingness to obey Christ's instructions enabled them to conceive. Once they committed themselves to conception (obeying Christ), they were able to reap a great harvest designed to bless their families, their neighbors, and their future brothers and sisters in Christ—throughout eternity.

Along with reaping a mighty harvest, Simon, James, and John's significant catch also symbolized the fruitful calling God had placed on their lives to draw, develop, and deliver a great number of souls into the Kingdom of Heaven. Through their openness and obedience to Christ, these future disciples were forever transformed from humble fishermen into prolific "fishers of men." It is important to note that, if they were going to be greatly used to bring others to Christ, they needed to *recognize, receive,* and *apply* the word of the Lord.

Just as God chose three exhausted fishermen to receive a seed that was designed to birth a blessing, you too can be chosen by your heavenly Father to receive a seed of promise. So I ask the question again, "Are you ready to receive your seed? Are you ovulating?"

If you are experiencing changes (maybe pressure, or even a slight pain), if you have a heightened sense of your surroundings, if you are encountering strong, Spirit-led desires—chances are, you are *ready to receive*. Chances are, *you are ready to conceive*.

ENDNOTES

1. Although this information is no longer available online, it was presented by Alejandro Boticelli of www.gambling911.com.

2. Barack Obama, *Dreams from My Father* (New York: Crown Publishers, a div. of Random House, Inc., 1995, 2004), 88-89.

3. Ibid., 95-96.

4. "Mother Teresa of Calcutta (1910–1997)," accessed March 30, 2012, http://www.vatican.va/news_services/liturgy/saints/ns_lit_doc_20031019_madre-teresa_en.html.

5. Kate Clifford Larson, "Harriet Tubman Biography," accessed March 30, 2012, http://www.harriettubmanbiography.com/.

CHAPTER 3

READY TO CONCEIVE

During the ovulation process, a mature egg is released from the ovary into the fallopian tube, where it awaits fertilization. Certain physical indicators have been associated with this process and, when present, they offer an accurate sense of when women are most fertile and likely to conceive. Primary signs, such as changes in the position of the cervix and in body temperature, may reveal that ovulation is about to occur and that it is time to intentionally engage in the activity leading to pregnancy.

Do you want to become pregnant with destiny? Are you sensing God wants to use you to deliver a promise that will fulfill His loving plan to save the world? If so, then it is time to examine your spiritual life to determine if you are in your fertile time. For the most part, the signals that point to ovulation are only obvious to the person who is experiencing this process. Therefore, it is extremely important for each of us to become familiar with the patterns that signal we are at the point in our cycle where we are ready to conceive.

Oftentimes, these subtle symptoms may be incorrectly attributed to many things, such as a cold, the flu, exhaustion, or heartburn. Since these symptoms mimic such common ailments, they can potentially be missed, overlooked, or ignored by busy, stressed-out, or inattentive people. Therefore, it is my hope that this chapter will help you identify, monitor, and understand the changes that accompany the time of your spiritual ovulation. By learning how to identify and comprehend these signs, you will become better prepared and, therefore, better able to conceive.

In order to understand *spiritual* ovulation, it is helpful to first understand what happens during *physical* ovulation. In the natural, conception begins as millions of sperm (seed) are released and race toward an individual egg. It takes time for the winner of this miraculous race to claim its victory by penetrating and passing through the mature egg's outer coating. If the egg or the seed are released too soon or too late, conception will not occur. Therefore, it is important that we remain informed, aware, and alert to the changes that occur in the spiritual realm so that we will be ready to receive our spiritual seed when it is released.

Since timing for this connection is critical, we cannot afford to wait until the moment of our spiritual ovulation before we increase our intimacy with God. As you read the next few pages, I urge you to familiarize yourself with your own spiritual timing in regard to your spiritual position and temperature. Now is the perfect time to enter your rightful place, with the right person, in order to receive a suitable seed that will set your destiny in motion.

> **Your desire must be joined with God's desire.**

As we near spiritual ovulation, our focus must move beyond the stage of just wanting God to please us. We must realize that what happens inside us affects what God is able to produce through us. Rather than wanting to go through the motions by ourselves, our desire must be joined with God's. We must allow Him to generate and nurture the idea or vision He has given us. Once we have matured enough to become fertile, we realize that, if we allow Him, in due time God will present the fruit of our spiritual womb as a gift to the world. Once our spiritual baby has entered the world, just as Hannah dedicated Samuel to the Lord's service (see 1 Sam. 1 and 2), we will want to do the same with our blessing.

POSITION

And the angel came in unto her, and said, Hail, thou that art highly favoured, the Lord is with thee: blessed art thou among women (Luke 1:28).

The cervix is the area in the woman's body that allows the semen to pass through into the uterus so that an egg can be fertilized. During a woman's monthly cycle, her cervix is initially hard and low. However, around her time of ovulation, the cervix shifts upward, softens, and opens. When pregnancy does not occur, the cervix only stays high for a day or two. However, if pregnancy does occur, the cervix tends to shift and stay in an upward position.

When there is a shift in our spiritual lives, we know we are ready to conceive. This shift will lift your thoughts out of the gutter and on to things that are lovely and pure. This shift will soften your heart toward all of God's creation and move you to a place of humility and gratitude. This shift will also open you up and allow you to hear and obey the voice of God. The image of shifting positions implies movement. The Bible offers several examples about how a perfect God uses imperfect but willing vessels to fill full of His glory and accomplish His holy purpose.

Mary's position was critical to the successful activation of the promised seed or, as the angel Gabriel named it, *"that holy thing"* (Luke 1:35). A brief synopsis of what the Bible reveals about Mary is captured by four descriptors: 1) she was an unmarried virgin; 2) she was highly favored and blessed; 3) she was humble; and 4) she was grateful to the Lord. Mary's position as a virgin was essential. The prophetic utterance was clear. Our King was to be born of a virgin (see Isa. 7:14). Had Mary already achieved the status of being someone's wife (a physically intimate partner), she would have been disqualified, by God's standards, to receive this particular assignment to carry the Seed of greatness and bring forth the means by which we are to be reconciled with God.

I can just imagine what was running through Mary's mind when she learned that she was chosen by God. *Why would God choose a simple girl like me? What is Joseph going to say? I know he is not going to believe me. He is going to think I betrayed him...that I was unfaithful. What are people going to think? I am poor and have no money. I am not ready to have a baby.*

In Luke 1:29, we are told that Mary was *"troubled at his saying"*; yet in spite of her mind being initially closed (for surely this is not how any of us would produce the Savior of the world), Mary lifted her eyes toward Heaven and shifted her body, mind, and soul into a place of openness. As she pressed into a place of surrender and humility, she raised herself into a fertile position. Only after she softly surrendered her will to God's will was she able to receive and eventually deliver what God had placed inside her.

The Scriptures also make it clear that Mary was a humble servant. Despite the announcement of her elevation, Mary did not brag, boast, or become haughty about being selected as the mother of her Lord. Her position *remained* one of humility. Though Mary was bold in her praise to God for what He had done, she never tried to personally benefit from the blessing. She took the stance that she had a small part to play in a bigger Kingdom agenda. Her spiritual posture did not change the entire time she was pregnant. Mary remained in position with a high praise, a soft heart, and an open spirit!

> **Through surrender and praise, the word of God will enter your spiritual womb.**

God also has a seed of greatness ready to deposit inside your spiritual womb that will benefit His Kingdom, but you cannot receive the seed if you are not in position to receive it or carry it. Only through the process of surrender, as evidenced by your praise, will you allow the word of God to enter into and be buried inside your spiritual womb. Just as the cervix must be lifted up, your spirit must also be lifted up. You must remain humble (not haughty) in order to receive the engrafted and prepared word of God. You must be lifted up in Him and understand that the God above wants to be the God in you.

In order to determine your ability to conceive, let's examine the position of your spiritual womb. Are you low, hard, and closed? Or are you high, open, and soft? Several factors may result in a low, hard, and closed position. For example, if you are detached, aloof, and indifferent; if you lack a spiritual covering (pastor); if you have problems with almost everyone in the church; or if you are bothered when others are blessed—then your spiritual position (lack of love, compassion, and faith), your physical position (no spiritual home), or your mental position (negative attitude) may be the very cause of your inability to receive what God has been trying to secure in your spirit.

On the other hand, if you can identify a time, or a pattern, in your development when you were located smack dab in the center of God's will; you clearly heard God's voice; or you willingly loved and served God's people (and plan) regardless of what you or others thought (or said)—then you have, most likely, experienced spiritual ovulation.

As we look inward to determine our position in regard to the condition of our fertility, it is imperative that we leave the official diagnoses to our heavenly Father (the divine Doctor on call). Ultimately, He has the final say regarding whether we are ready to conceive or whether we require any number of fertility treatments. Just like Mary, we may think we are unworthy of the assignment. All we have to do is show up in God's office, tell Him all about our troubles, wait for His diagnosis, and comply with His prescription.

As you continue to read this book, I join you, in prayer, asking God to orchestrate a supernatural shift in your life. Take a moment to reflect, repent, and reconcile your heart, mind, and soul. Position yourself to receive. You may have unknowingly let your guard down and allowed the enemy to infiltrate your thoughts to such an extent that you do not believe God is able. If this is the case, ask God to forgive you. You must also repent if a negative attitude has caused you to let down your brothers and sisters in Christ. Know that you serve an awesome and mighty God who is faithful and just to forgive you. Remember, the correct position, beloved, is ultimately one of surrender. Today, surrender your will, your thoughts, your desires, and your entire being to God's will. Decide to come out of your situation with your hands lifted high in *praise!* Know that God will certainly turn your situation around. Get ready to receive! Get ready to change positions! Get ready to conceive!

TEMPERATURE

Temperature also plays a significant role in assessing whether a woman's body is ready to conceive. When a woman is having trouble conceiving, her body or basal temperature is often measured to determine whether she is in the correct phase for receiving the seed, and, more importantly, for the *implantation* of that seed. When a woman takes the time to chart her temperature every day for months on end, it is because she is of the mindset to conceive. In order to ensure the accuracy of her records, she must check her temperature at the same time each morning, before she even gets out of bed or utters a single word.

What about us? Do we check our spiritual temperature before we get out of bed each morning? Before we speak to any other human being, do we ask God to guide our footsteps—to lead us not into temptation and to deliver us from evil?

Typically, a basal chart will reveal ups and downs in a woman's temperature. Initially, these fluctuations are slight; however, when ovulation occurs, there is a dramatic dip, immediately followed by an even higher rise in temperature. When the egg is ready to be fertilized, the woman's temperature remains at its peak for a number of consecutive days.

Most of us will agree that our road to spiritual maturity has also been paved with ups and downs. Unfortunately, we often fail to see the significance of what appears to be the lowest moment in our walk with God. I say this because of the many sermons I have heard regarding how we have disappointed God and how our lack of faith caused the sad or hard things we face. Similarly, as Job's friends did, how many times have we speculated about what our sister or brother did to bring about some tragedy?

Here lies an important revelation that we need to grasp. At the lowest point on the chart, ovulation has occurred. Similarly, when it looks like we are at our lowest point, God often uses this setting to orchestrate a blessing or plan that will bring glory to His name and His Kingdom. However, since we are not always mindful of God's actions and plans, we often miss this point and assume we are hitting rock bottom rather than getting ready to soar to the top.

> **God often orchestrates a blessing or plan that brings glory to Him.**

We know that we are at our most fertile point when our immediate response to life's circumstances is to bow down in prayer and worship before the Lord, and remain there until we receive His life-sustaining seed (information). So, when all hell breaks loose around us and we feel like we have hit rock bottom, how should we respond? We should encourage ourselves in the Lord!

60

In First Samuel chapter 30 we read that David and his men wept until they had no strength left to weep after discovering that the Amalekites had burned Ziklag and stolen their wives, sons, and daughters, taking them into captivity. Adding to David's distress, his men's grief for their missing loved ones produced rumors of stoning David, their once-admired leader. Verses 6-8 tell us that David responded to the threat of attack by encouraging himself in the Lord and asking God for direction.

Unfortunately, we Christians often allow our experiences to affect our temperature (feelings or attitudes), rather than letting our temperature impact how we respond to our experiences. Just as a woman's temperature rises significantly above the other high temperatures she has previously experienced in her cycle, our spiritual temperature should also go higher. Though we face a variety of ups and downs, we need to rise significantly above our circumstances and sustain our spiritual temperature. We need to walk in purpose so that nothing can rattle us or take us off course.

It is interesting to note that the words "temperature" and "temperance" originate from the Latin word *temperare,* which means to moderate, be moderate in action, thought, or feeling. Temperance suggests the ability to habitually moderate our emotions and our behaviors. Rather than being tempered by the Spirit of the Lord, we, too often, allow ourselves to be tempered by money problems, relationship problems, and a host of other situations we are faced with on a daily basis. Hebrews 4 instructs us to make every effort to enter into the rest that God has promised. Because we can trust that whatever God provides is complete, we can completely rest our bodies, minds, and souls in His good and perfect will. In addition, since Jesus provides us with daily rest, through faith, all we have to do is believe in His provision and then walk therein by the power of the Holy Spirit.

When a person neglects to manage his or her temper and allows his or her spiritual temperature to become too hot (from anger) or too cold (from disinterest or lack of faith), conception will not occur. Therefore, we cannot ignore how our mental and spiritual attitude factors into the conception process. Psalm 1:2 states, *"But his delight is in the law of the LORD; and in his law doth he meditate day and night."* This Word teaches us that we are personally responsible for receiving God's seed with the proper frame of mind. If we fail to do this, we risk the chance of our seed being burned (too hot) or frozen (too cold) by our feelings and emotional responses to life!

Therefore, throughout your daily activities, as you enter settings that are suitable for procreation (worship services, workplaces, or classrooms), you must come with the intention of receiving a word—of instruction. Otherwise, you will never conceive. As you enter sanctified or hallowed places, you come needing, expecting, and willing to hear a word from the Lord. Even as you face the inevitable difficulties that are part of life, you must be able to manage and control your feelings and emotions. Otherwise, you risk becoming despondent or spiritually depressed with a hardened heart or a lowered level of expectation. If you allow yourself to be negatively affected or distracted by worries, fears, and challenges, you may prevent yourself from receiving the positive, life-changing word that God designed specifically for you.

Please understand that I am not referring to individuals who come to church, work, or school in a grief-stricken state. Remember, we often receive our blessings when we are at our lowest point. However, I am referring to the saints who *choose* to be miserable;

choose to come to church, work, or school in a miserable state; and *choose* to manipulate those around them in order to legitimize their own misery. I am speaking of those with hardened hearts, hot tempers, or cold (defeated) attitudes, who have allowed their characters to rise or fall beyond life-sustaining temperatures due to bitterness, jealousy, or anger. Bitterness causes you to be barren, unable to conceive and give birth to dreams and destinies.

With an improper spiritual temperature, a person can hear the word of God and receive instruction, but not have the ability to apply the information. With an improper spiritual temperature, praise can become irritating when God's holy name is exalted. Instead of echoing the preacher's encouraging words and allowing God's liberating Spirit to flow and transform, the untempered (unrestrained) spirit repeats, "It's too hard," "I can't do it," and "Things will never change."

As human beings created by God, we are certain to experience trials and tribulations that occasionally affect our emotions for a season. However, I mean to caution individuals who experience trouble that they can and should expect God to turn their situation around. Hold on to Psalm 30:5b, which encourages us to remember that *"weeping may endure for a night, but joy cometh in the morning."* We must fully understand that God has all the power to turn anything around, to turn mourning into dancing and to exchange peace for sadness (see Ps. 30:11). We should be able to conceive—even at a loved one's funeral with tears running down our faces.

Remember how a woman is most fertile when her low temperature is followed immediately by a spike, which remains at its peak for a number of consecutive days? Well, Christians are in their most fertile time when they are able to respond to depressing, painful, or aggravating circumstances with a realization that God is in control. Once they have that realization cemented in their spirits, they can then immediately enter into a place of praise and remain there for the duration of their assignment.

Oftentimes, we feel our circumstances are so overwhelming that it may appear that God hasn't equipped us with the ability to handle the misery of our condition. However, beloved, that is simply not true. As Christians, we must understand that we are peculiar people. We must hold on to God's unchanging hand and know that the Bible says we can do all things through Christ (see Phil. 4:13).

Frequently, as it relates to destiny, people find themselves in a desert place when they try to handle things without the help of God. Any task, whether it is easy, mediocre, or difficult, can only be accomplished through Jesus Christ. You can *overcome* stress IN HIS NAME; you can *deal* with death IN HIS NAME; and you can *conquer* sickness IN HIS NAME. However, if you begin to echo the lies of the adversary, you will never conceive the things of God. Therefore, take courage, because *you are not the abused of Satan—you are the bride of Christ!*

The good thing that was committed unto you and is kept by the Holy Spirit to dwell in you will give you the strength, courage, and wisdom for another breakthrough and another harvest. Everything God needs to carry you to your next level is already in you. You just have to make up your mind to find your pleasure in what God says is true, rather than allowing yourself to get bogged down by the facts that your current condition naturally suggests. After all, God is not limited to operating in the natural. His most amazing results occur when He operates in the supernatural. So, comfort and delight yourself in the law of the Lord. Meditate on it day and night, for that is where your blessing lies (see Ps. 1:2).

And when she saw him, she was troubled at his saying, and cast in her mind what manner of salutation this should be (Luke 1:29).

It is only natural for us to be troubled by a seemingly "impossible" word. Remember, when Mary first heard the seed, *"thou shalt conceive,"* she was still a virgin. The Bible says that her natural state caused her to be *"troubled"* by the word the angel spoke to her. Often when God gives us a seemingly "impossible" word, instead of rejoicing, we get discouraged. Since it is easier to receive a word of possibility, like Mary, we tend to stress out when we receive a word of impossibility. However, during these seemingly impossible times, we must remember that His ways are not our ways (see Isa. 55:8), and that all things are possible through Christ who strengthens us.

> **Adapt your thoughts, feelings, and perceptions to joy and praise—or risk your destiny.**

No matter how daunting, challenging, or fearful Gabriel's announcement sounded to Mary, if she was to fulfill her destiny to carry the Savior of the world in her belly and birth the King of kings and Lord of lords, she would have to embrace her seed of destiny and praise God for selecting her to have His Son. We must mimic Mary's remarks when she responded, *"Behold the handmaid of the Lord; be it unto me according to thy word"* (Luke 1:38a). Just as Mary quickly adjusted her attitude and frame of mind, we, too, must adapt our thoughts, feelings, perceptions, and overall state of mind to one of joy and praise; otherwise, we risk the conception of our destiny.

> *But the fruit of the Spirit is love, joy, peace, longsuffering, gentleness, goodness, faith, meekness, temperance: against such there is no law* (Galatians 5:22-23).

The Bible reminds us to sanctify ourselves; to be content in all things; to count it all joy; and to be steadfast, unmovable, and always abounding in the work of the Lord.[1] In spite of what goes on in our lives, we must strive to be unmoved by external factors while allowing the power of the Spirit of God to have His way in and through us. We must strive to rise above, and stay above, our limited ability to see, to know, or to act.

I'll let you in on a little secret. When a woman's body temperature stays high for a consecutive number of days, if she becomes pregnant, those high temperature days turn into months. Throughout her entire pregnancy, her temperature remains elevated. As we learn to rely on the One who is all-seeing, all-knowing, and all-powerful, our internal spiritual gauge should also be stuck on high—high praises, high hopes, high places in God. Similarly, one way you can know if your intimacy with God has resulted in pregnancy is by checking your spiritual temperature.

The root word for "temperature" and "temperance" ("temper") comes from the Latin word *tempus,* which means time or season. This brings us to the final section of this chapter. Thus far we have learned that when we want to conceive, there are telltale signs that indicate if we are ovulating or fertile. As I stated earlier, we look for these signs primarily to let us know when it is *time* to actively engage in the conception process. Why would we need to know the proper time? It's simply because *timing truly matters!*

Timing Is Everything!

And in the sixth month the angel Gabriel was sent from God unto a city of Galilee, named Nazareth, to a virgin espoused to a man whose name was Joseph, of the house of David; and the virgin's name was Mary (Luke 1:26-27).

In Matthew 1:20, Joseph had a dream. In the dream, God chose the perfect time to tell Joseph that he should not be afraid to take Mary as his wife. Dreams such as Joseph's can also contain seed for our destiny. How we respond to these dreams is very important.

When living in West Virginia, one year we spent the Fourth of July holiday in Washington, D.C. While there, my brother-in-law asked me to accompany him to the Board of Education so that he could apply for a job. When they found out that I was overqualified to teach special education, they offered me a position. Because I was working on my doctoral degree and was already teaching and preaching in West Virginia, I declined the offer. In fact, when I told my wife about the job, we laughed because she was also busy earning her degree in West Virginia.

Upon returning home, you can imagine my surprise upon awaking from a dream, only a few days later, and realizing that God was telling me to leave the comfort of my home state and move to our nation's capital. In the dream, I was alone in a barren valley. It was filled with trees that were as huge as giant sequoias. Though the trees were not dead, they were infertile and did not have any leaves. It was as if I was in a petrified situation.

I knew it was not good for me to be there, and I needed to get out of that barren place. However, no matter how hard I tried, I just couldn't make it out on my own. Tired and discouraged, as I looked for a way out, I noticed a beautiful white steed running in a full gallop on the top edge of the mountain range. I had never seen such a beautiful and awesome horse. He was running so fast that I asked myself, *What is that horse doing up there, just running and running?*

Then the horse ran around to the other side of the valley and started coming down the hill. When I realized he was headed straight toward me, I panicked and tried to climb up one of the desolate, towering trees. The branches were as flat as a plank floor and must have been fifteen feet wide. I only made it up a few branches when the horse jumped onto the branch I was on. Trying to get away, I fell back and landed on my left side.

There was a little tree stump sticking out of the ground that bruised my ribs. The injury left me barely able to move. Stunned, I watched the steed jump out of the tree and run over to me. It then slung its beautiful mane down toward me, to let me know that it wanted to help me up. Realizing God had sent that amazing animal to rescue me from the fruitless valley, I reached up and grabbed its mane. I held on with all my strength as that high-spirited stallion whipped his mane around, flipped me onto its back, and carried me up out of the valley.

When we arrived on top of the mountain, I noticed that the sun was warm and bright and that everything outside the valley was lush and beautiful. I got down off the horse, but he followed me wherever I went. I couldn't shake my rescuer. No matter where I'd walk, I'd turn around and think to myself, *He's still here. He's still here.* And then I woke up.

I woke up to a phone call, only to find out that the school where I taught burned down that night. Since I was one of the last ones hired, I knew I would lose my job—and I knew the Lord was sending me to D.C. God used the dream to show me that if I tried to remain in West Virginia, my endeavors would be fruitless. In fact, I sensed that He had already chosen someone else to fruitfully minister in that region. God gave me that particular dream at that particular time to show me that, just because I was birthed in West Virginia, I was not meant to continually labor and abundantly harvest there. *Timing is everything!*

Likewise, your place of birth may not be your place of abundance. When God moves us from our place of birth, we can trust that He will lead us to a place where we are capable of producing an even greater harvest. When we are removed from all that is familiar and comfortable, we tend to rely more on God to provide us with our needs. Even Jesus was not destined to produce an abundant harvest in Nazareth, the place of His birth. In fact, He was scorned in His own hometown. In order to produce a life-sustaining, overflowing harvest that would bless the world, as Jesus ministered throughout Judea and Samaria, He was continually tested and tried.

Since West Virginia was no longer where I needed to be, the Lord impressed upon me that time was of the essence and it was imperative that I move immediately. I am happy to say that my quick response to that dream seed put me on the path to a satisfying and successful ministry in the nation's capital. Again, seed comes in many forms, and responding to the seed will take us to the path of our destiny. I repeat, *timing is everything!*

Both *spiritual* and *physical* conceiving and birthing involve timing. During the process of *physical* conception, there are only a few days during the month when a woman can conceive. No matter how many times a seed is sown during a given month, if the seed is not received during this time frame, conception will not occur. Just like the physical conception process illustrates, so it is also true with receiving a word from God—especially a word of destiny. Therefore, *timing truly matters!*

When God released the seed that changed the world, there was a set time for the announcement, the impartation, and the arrival. It was the sixth month when God sent the angel Gabriel. At the time the angel arrived, Mary was still a virgin and engaged to be married. The Lord could have waited to overshadow Mary after she had already married Joseph, but Jesus had to be born of a virgin. *"Therefore the Lord himself shall give you a sign; Behold, a virgin shall conceive, and bear a son, and shall call his name Immanuel"* (Isa. 7:14).

Indeed, it is in the Immaculate Conception that the miracle has its power! It was in the *timing* of the conception that the miracle was manifested. The Bible says, *"To every thing there is a season, and a time to every purpose under the heaven"* (Eccl. 3:1). Just as Mary's circumstances (her favor with God, her virginity, and her fiancé's genealogy) were in time with the purpose of God, our lives can also be in time and in tune with the Lord so that we can receive a powerful, life-changing word.

If a woman is truly in tune with her body, she can sense when she is ovulating. She may feel a little anxious, her physical senses may become keener, her desire for intimacy may increase, and she may actually feel the egg release. Whatever the symptoms, she knows and senses that the "time of the month" is on its way. Likewise, spiritually, we can sense a blessing coming.

> **If you are not ready or sanctified in your heart, you will not be in God's timing.**

In order to sense the blessing coming, we must be in tune with the Spirit of God, and, as I previously stated, we must approach the throne of God with expectation. When we go to church, we must attend expecting to hear a word from the Lord. We must be faithful and in tune with the rhythm of the Holy Ghost. The Bible instructs to *"be ready always"* and to *"sanctify the Lord God in your hearts"* (1 Pet. 3:15a). If we are not ready or have not sanctified the Lord in our hearts, we will not be in tune with the timing of God.

To sanctify the Lord in our hearts is to set apart the Lord in our hearts so that He can make us holy and acceptable before Him. In order to do this, we must ask God to be our Lord and our Savior. In other words, we must give God free reign over our lives by asking Jesus to forgive us of our sins and asking the Holy Spirit to guide us in our daily decisions. As we move forward, from moment to moment, we must take care that we do not allow anyone or anything to take God's sovereign place.

We must prepare ourselves by passionately pursuing God throughout the day during our times of private and public devotion. As we pray, read the Bible, and worship Him with music and the preached word, we must humble ourselves, thanking Him for His goodness and mercy, and acknowledge His greatness. It is imperative that we submit to His wisdom, rely on His power, trust His faithfulness, love Him, obey Him, honor Him, and give Him all the glory. Otherwise, the seed *will* be sown, but we will not conceive.

> *And Mary said, Behold the handmaid of the Lord;*
> *be it unto me according to thy word...* (Luke 1:38).

As we take another look at Luke 1:38, we see that Mary's declaration of acceptance shows that she clearly understood that in order to receive the word God was sowing in her spirit, her thinking had to change. Mary—not God—had to transform her troubled spirit into one of godly acceptance, and ultimately one of praise. Shortly thereafter, Mary boldly declared, *"My soul doth magnify the Lord, and my spirit hath rejoiced in God my Saviour"* (Luke 1:46-47). Mary's attitude of praise allowed her spirit to accept the word that the Lord imparted. Mary's attitude allowed God's word to transform her natural ability to give birth into a supernatural, miraculous fulfillment of a prophetic promise.

Since God wants to sow something into your life and into your spirit that will bless both you and the world, it is vital that you press to remain consistently ready and open to receive your seed and embrace whatever He is saying as it pertains to the fulfillment of your destiny. In order to successfully deliver a healthy promise, you must fully recognize that there is a set time and season for your word (blessing) to manifest. You must not let the timing of the manifestation distract you from receiving the seed, which is the word of God. You must not hinder the word of God from inhabiting your soul and your spirit, or from letting it grow and mature into what God has purposed.

Now we know all about the miracle of birthing what God set us apart to do before we were born (see Jer. 1:5). This *knowing* is revealed to us out of a deeply personal and intimate relationship with God. We know that we are *"created in Christ Jesus to do* [produce, birth, deliver] *good works, which God prepared* [planned] *in advance for us to do"* (Eph. 2:10 NIV), so that we may live productive lives (see Titus 3:14 NIV). We know that the plans He has for us are plans to prosper us, to give us hope and a future (see Jer. 29:11). Just as Paul prayed for the church at Colosse, we should also be filled with the knowledge of God's will in order that we may live lives worthy of the Lord and please Him—bearing fruit and growing even more in the knowledge of Christ (see Col. 1:10 NIV).

The next chapter discusses how feelings of inadequacy, impatience, and self-importance can deceive us. I will explain how the enemy uses these tools to get us to live lives unworthy of the Lord and behave contrary to the knowledge that God supplies us with everything we will need to birth greatness. If we buy the lie, we are sure to displease God, destroy our fruits, and diminish our intimacy with our Lord. That's *risky business!*

ENDNOTE

1. See Joshua 3:5, Philippians 4:11, James 1:2, and First Corinthians 15:58.

CHAPTER 4

PREGNANT BY THE WRONG PERSON

For they have taken of their daughters for themselves, and for their sons: so that the holy seed have mingled themselves with the people of those lands: yea, the hand of the princes and rulers hath been chief in this trespass (Ezra 9:2).

We have discussed how we are partly responsible for creating and managing the terms and conditions under which the birth of our destiny is set in motion. We have also suggested that our character and diligence sustain us in the process of achieving our destiny. This, of course, is easier said than done. I once preached a sermon about the weapons of spiritual warfare against us being, first, ourselves; next, the folks around us; and finally, spiritual wickedness in high places. In Paul's second letter to Timothy, he warns his spiritual son to *"flee the evil desires of youth and pursue righteousness, faith, love, and peace, along with those who call on the Lord out of a pure heart"* (2 Tim. 2:22 NIV). In other words, Timothy was instructed to actively separate himself from his earthly nature (represented by death of self, and a new life now hidden with Christ in God), and to position himself alongside others who were seeking God with a pure heart.

In the fifth chapter of Matthew, Jesus tells us that the pure in heart will see God. Purity is the prerequisite if we want God to reveal Himself in our family, ministry, and all areas of our lives. Throughout God's Word we are taught to circumcise our hearts, to fix God's words in our hearts, to incline our hearts to the Lord, that our hearts must be fully committed, to understand with our hearts, and to purify our hearts.[1]

Psalm 24:4 tells us that the pure in heart do *"not* [lift] *up* [their] *soul to an idol"* (NKJV). This means that the pure in heart do not put their emotions, thoughts, motivations, courage, actions, worship, or trust in anyone, or anything, above the one and only living God. This chapter highlights some of the perils of trying to satisfy the lust of the eyes, the lust of the flesh, and the pride of self by putting other gods before the one true God. I pray that you will arrive at the same conclusion that I have—promiscuity is *risky business!*

> **Purity is the prerequisite if you want God
> to reveal Himself in all areas of your life.**

If we truly love Jesus, the very idea of disappointing, hurting, or angering Him ought to cause us great sadness. When we consider the long-term, life-changing risks associated with what I call spiritual promiscuity, we should conclude that there is no momentary thrill or attraction worth these risks. Though the costs are not always monetary and we may avoid immediate payment for our risky behavior, we may be sure that the eventual cost of infidelity and betrayal is quite real.

In our culture, a person who indiscriminately associates with many sexual partners is defined as promiscuous. Promiscuity is the opposite of purity. It emphasizes frequent, casual, and random encounters to satisfy self-indulgent sexual (or other fleshly) desires. By nature, as promiscuity violates our relationships, it can't help but negatively affect our future and the future of those whose destinies are tied to our own. Violating our commitment to the covenant relationship we have with God threatens the fulfillment of God's promises for our lives.

This language and image of promiscuity, as it relates to destiny, is not unfamiliar to the body of Christ. The imagery of prostitution, representing Israel's unfaithfulness to the God of their covenant, is common in the prophetic books, especially the books of Ezra, Jeremiah, and Hosea. The Old Testament consistently portrays Israel's betrayal of the commitment they made to God as they worshiped graven images and idols. The result of their promiscuity, hedonism, and infidelity was either the delay, the denial, or the destruction of their destiny.

The ninth chapter of the book of Ezra describes how the people of Israel entered into unholy unions with idol worshipers. The prophet tells us that God provoked Cyrus, king of Persia, into allowing the nation of Israel to rebuild the Temple of God. However, during the midst of rebuilding, it was discovered that the people of Israel intermarried with their non-Jewish neighbors. According to the conditions of their covenant, this act of infidelity had been forbidden by God, since the marriages turned Israel away from following Him and led them into worshiping the false gods of their neighbors (see Deut. 7).

The etymology of the word "promiscuous" sheds light on how promiscuity affects destiny. The prefix *pro* means forward or before, and the suffix *miscere* means to mix. In essence, promiscuity is the disorderly mixing, mingling, or confusion of people and things and is typically characterized by indiscriminate sexual encounters. It is often manifested when a man or woman, guided by his or her lusts, wanders from one place or partner to another. Promiscuity creates chaotic linkages among people and circumstances, which establishes the backdrop for intense mischief and confusion.

In the natural, sex establishes physical and soulful connections, even when there is a clear statement that the intent of the interaction is only for a momentary hookup. The promiscuous person behaves as if these connections will have little or no impact on the lives of the individuals involved. However, as such individuals repeatedly seek out and engage in multiple sexual encounters, chaos abounds as people, places, and conditions become unhealthily mingled.

As we examine the history of the children of Israel (the children of the promise, the chosen seed), we repeatedly observe a pattern of turning toward idol worship, followed by penalties, and finally repentance. Initially, Israel entered into a solemn covenant with Jehovah, whereby they accepted Him as the one true God and pledged faithful service to Him (see Exod. 19:3-8; 20:2-5). Yet time after time, we read how their broken vows and their tendency to stray from their heavenly Father kept them from receiving their promised inheritance.

What prompts us to leave our God-ordained position and abort our God-given assignment? What causes us to disregard our covenant commitments to seek affection and attention from encounters that are, at best, insignificant and, at worst, harmful to us and those we love? Simply put, we, like the children of Israel, are spurred to promiscuity by impatience, restlessness, and a failure to communicate with God. After all, that is what prompted the Israelites to fashion the golden calf and delay their promise. Immaturity caused them to imagine that Moses' return to his people was delayed while he communicated with God on Mount Sinai. Exodus 32:1 reads:

> *And when the people saw that Moses delayed to come down out of the mount, the people gathered themselves together unto Aaron, and said unto him, Up, make us gods, which shall go before us; for as for this Moses, the man that brought us up out of the land of Egypt, we wot not what is become of him.*

There are other reasons why we stray. These include interpreting the peace and quiet place of God as boring and uninspiring; or believing that living the Christian life is equal to settling for less. Although we are not perfect and will have occasions to stumble or fall, the possibility of not experiencing the fullness of a purposeful, meaningful, and long-lasting life in the land of promise ought to help keep our hearts turned toward the only true Lover of our souls.

How can we experience the life of promise that God created for each of us? We can start by firmly committing to the ministry where our promise was designed to be conceived. Being committed to the spiritual covering and donor God assigned to discharge the seed of your destiny will result in your destiny being properly conceived, developed, and delivered in due season. If we spiritually wander away from a preordained partner (the pastor) and place (the church) that our heavenly Father chose for the birthing of our destiny, the promise placed inside us will become skewed (promise-skew-ity). Invariably, the skewing of our promise will lead to all kinds of mix-ups and confusions, which can have devastating and life-destroying effects. Wandering off and turning away from our intended partner and place of growth puts God's promises for our lives in jeopardy. We risk becoming pregnant by the wrong person or contracting an infection, which could cause complications with conception or problems with our pregnancy.

PREGNANT BY THE WRONG PERSON

Imagine the resounding joy in the heart of a person who has just learned that he or she is about to have a baby. Then, imagine the sorrow and disheartening feeling of those who are torn between the excitement of conception and the pain of knowing that they are pregnant by, or with, the wrong person—someone outside the marriage relationship. Tragically, such a person is facing a future that lacks order, since the wrong father or mother of the baby is not ideally suited to parent the child.

Most of us have at least heard of a situation where a married woman gets pregnant by someone other than her spouse, but tries to pass the child off as the husband's child. When it starts to become obvious that the child does not walk, talk, or act like other members of the family, or that the child possesses a distinctive gift or talent, accusations begin to fly and the harmony of the home begins to deteriorate. Soon, even people familiar with the family also recognize that the child, born from another's seed, is the product of deception and unfaithfulness. The ability of the family to thrive, both individually and collectively, is threatened by the sham. Tragically, the critical support network of family and friends is frayed by anger and disappointment.

When we talk about being pregnant by the wrong person from a spiritual perspective, clarity causes us to acknowledge that *improper relationships* can interrupt the flow of God's plan for our lives. In order to give birth to destiny, we must first enter into a covenant whereby we commit to flow within the current of love and faith that God has designed for us. Doing this will bring stability, serenity, and peace into our lives.

> **Improper relationships can interrupt the flow of God's plan for your life.**

Conversely, agitation and confusion are the result of operating outside God's intended current of love and faith. This agitation can delay God's promise, or even cause us to miscarry our destiny. This disruption of purpose and redirection of focus, energy, and resources usually begins when we enter the wrong place at the wrong time or venture into a situation designed for someone else.

UNEQUALLY YOKED

I know the significance of disobeying the principle of being equally yoked; I've had to eliminate my interactions with certain people and stop spending time in certain places. As you can imagine, this pulling away has led to misunderstandings, hurt feelings, and frustration. If it were not for the grace of God, these inappropriate hookups could have sidetracked or derailed the divine plan for my life.

There are similar consequences when we wander carelessly into relationships that challenge our code of spiritual beliefs and behaviors and entice us to question their relevance. Soon, of our own accord, we seek to modify or alter our spiritual code of conduct in various settings (our ministries, churches, homes, jobs) and in numerous ways, which represent a noticeable departure from the norm.

Let me clearly state that I am not encouraging spiritual stagnation. However, I would suggest that the new spiritual revelation, or an evolved spiritual understanding, happens by an orderly move of the Holy Spirit, at its appointed time, for a particular purpose, and to a specific people or person. If God isn't the source of the revelation and the instigator of change, destiny can be compromised. This is why it is critical that we only become spiritually pregnant by those who know the context in which we have to carry out our assignment and who, most likely, are at the heart of the spiritual network that God has assigned to strengthen our ability to accomplish divine purpose.

Previously, we discussed the romance between the pulpit and the pews and how the preached Word enters our wombs and inseminates us with purpose, vision, and greatness. If we develop a proper relationship with our pastor and move in harmony with our shepherd, then the Word of God, as preached by the man (or woman) of God, can enter into our spirits and bring forth everything that God has called us to birth, to be, or to do. If we are connected to a particular ministry, then we are assigned to that pastor's vision. If we wander off to other ministries and conceive, we may not only return home pregnant by the wrong person, but we also will likely expect our pastor to care for and nurture the gift growing inside us. When our pastor is unable to do so, an undesirable situation arises. Most likely, we will be left bearing the burden of a pregnancy alone—without the company and support of the proper father.

Imagine the excitement your pastor will experience when he or she discovers that you have conceived. Now imagine his or her disheartening pain upon the realization that he or she is not the parent, and that your pregnancy is a result of your spiritually promiscuous behavior. A pastor can always tell when members wander somewhere else and become pregnant. They return with a different perspective or perception. They try to bring back something from another ministry to implement at home. They boast about what God has done in their spirits while at the other ministry. The word they receive at the other ministry may be a good word, since it is God's word. However it may not be the word they need to establish, nourish, and develop the specific plans that God ordained for them before the beginning of time.

Although the idea that saints receive while away from their home church might be a good idea, it might not be the *right* idea for their home ministry at that particular season. Soon, frustration is sure to develop. Next, criticism for their spiritual father or pastor and that ministry is likely to take root. All of a sudden, the wandering parishioners start *claiming* that their pastor is not "in the flow of the spirit." In reality, they are experiencing the effects of their promiscuity.

Impregnated by another ministry, they erroneously expect their pastor to care for and nurture someone else's seed. In situations like this, the ministry they have casually related with may be in a season of reaping, while the ministry they are committed to is in a season of sowing. Sadly, when they return to their home church, they are spiritually frustrated because they now feel like they should be reaping while, in all actuality, they are supposed to be in a season of sowing. This example is meant to convey the types of danger we face when we have a wandering eye and wandering ways.

ROOTED AND GROUNDED

Remember, beloved, in order to birth promise and destiny, you must be *rooted* and *grounded*. The Bible commands us to be steadfast, unmovable, always abounding in the work of the Lord (see 1 Cor. 15:58). Stick and stay and pray! Don't be a temple prostitute! Be faithful, fixed in place, and receive your seed. Your commitment to the ministry where promise was purposed to be conceived and your commitment to the spiritual father or mother of your seed will pave the way to the healthy delivery of the promise prepared specifically for you.

It is interesting to note that people who are promiscuous in their personal relationships are usually promiscuous in every aspect of their lives. They are unfaithful at home, on the job, and in their ministry. They are not devoted or committed to vision, purpose, or destiny. Promoted and provoked by the lust of their flesh, they stray away from their assigned places. In regard to their experiences (family, professional, and worship), they tend to function by how they *feel* or *want to feel*, rather than by what they *know*.

Because promiscuous behavior puts us at risk for becoming pregnant by a *stranger* and creates a whole host of unintended outcomes, we should *know* the person with whom we are intimate. To *know* is to be or feel certain of the truth or accuracy of some fact; to grasp in the mind with clarity or certainty. We should be mindful of those with whom we are intimate. Though it may be lawful in the earthly sense to have sexual relations or conversations with whomever we choose, we should keep in mind that we have to live with the consequences of the decisions we make. In the realm of both the spiritual and the natural, understand that we should *know* the person with whom we are intimate and by whom we allow ourselves to become impregnated.

The word "know" as used in certain Scriptures means an intimate relationship between a man and a woman, such as when Adam "knew" Eve (Gen. 4:1). In the King James Version, the phrase "he knew" literally means "he had sexual intercourse with." Sexual union represents oneness and knowledge of the other person. Sexual intercourse is the most intimate act between a man and woman. It is the glue that seals social, physical, emotional, and spiritual attachments. That is why God has reserved it for marriage alone.

Because knowing someone via this binding process can create such sticky situations, men must carefully choose where they sow their seed and women must carefully choose who they allow to release seed into their lives. Any time there is any level of intimacy (whether through conversation, sexual intercourse, partnership, relationship, and/or fellowship), we open ourselves up to being subjected to or influenced by another person's agenda and spiritual DNA.

From both a physical and spiritual aspect, if we partake in promiscuous behavior, we risk becoming pregnant, infected, or controlled by someone we do not know. Therefore, from a Kingdom perspective, it is not incidental that Scripture instructs that we are to "know" those who labor among us (see 1 Thess. 5:12). Knowing the gifts that the members and overseers of our local church body possess enhances our spiritual growth and improves the likelihood of the conception and the birth of our destiny.

MIND MATTERS IN MATTERS OF THE HEART

For it is from within, out of a person's heart, that evil thoughts come... (Mark 7:21 NIV).

When becoming pregnant after engaging in spiritual adultery or promiscuity, we may find ourselves trying to birth destiny as a single parent. As many single parents can attest, trying to hold a family together without the physical, psychological, and spiritual support of the other parent can be quite difficult. Typically, both children and parents of single-parent families must overcome greater obstacles than two-parent families, such as financial difficulties, educational barriers, and emotional struggles. All of these issues can have a dramatic effect on the health of each family member. One initial health risk that stems from spiritual promiscuity is the increased possibility of contracting infections. As a result, our ability to carry and deliver the potential and promise that resides within us is greatly impacted.

Adultery and promiscuity are acts of the carnal-minded. Saints who strive to be spiritual-minded allow the Holy Spirit to influence their thoughts, conscience, emotions, and will. On the other hand, carnal-minded individuals are less concerned with matters that pertain to life in Christ than they are with worldly affairs. Self-centeredness (carnality), instead of God-centeredness (spirituality), takes over like an infection and attacks the body. As the flesh dominates the spirit, the capacity to receive and obey God's directives is limited. In the natural, infection impacts fertility, pregnancy, and delivery. Likewise, in the spiritual, our ability to conceive, carry, and bring forth destiny is compromised by infection.

The Bible tells us that spiritual-mindedness brings life and peace (see Rom. 8:6), while carnal-mindedness leads to chaos and death. When we hear the acronym STD, we generally associate it with the term "Sexually Transmitted Disease." STDs are viral or bacterial infections[2] spread from person to person through intimate contact and are often the result of sexually promiscuous behavior. Infections can have a devastating effect on fertility, conception, pregnancy, and delivery.

For this teaching, STD will represent a Spiritually Transmitted Disease. When we seek out frequent, casual, and random affairs of the heart, we increase the likelihood that our thinking will become infected with incorrect (diseased) ideas, or as Joyce Meyers puts it, we have "stinking thinking." Once our minds, hearts, and souls have been infected, disobedience is sure to follow. As the root of disobedience begins to grow inside us, alienation from our God also gains ground. The farther off-track our thinking becomes, the greater the risk is that our delivery date will be delayed, or even that our destiny will be spontaneously aborted.

Medically, if a mother is infected with a STD, her pregnancy can be accompanied by many dangerous complications. One common complication that can occur is a tubal pregnancy, also referred to as an ectopic pregnancy. Remember, in a normal pregnancy, once conception has occurred, the fertilized egg usually travels from the ovary to the uterus, where it is safely embedded in the womb and begins to grow. However, if a STD infects the fallopian tube, it may become blocked. When this happens, the fertilized egg becomes implanted in the tube and continues to develop there. These pregnancies are never viable. In fact, tubal pregnancies are the number one cause of death in women during their first trimester of pregnancy. To be pregnant in the wrong place can cause death to both the destiny and the destiny carrier.

In order for a fertilized egg to survive, it must reach the womb and attach to a healthy endometrial lining, which is free of scarring and disease. The growth and thickening of our spiritual endometrial lining occurs as part of the God-inspired conception process. For life to be created and sustained, we must respond to the commands (thoughts) of God with love and obedience. Jeremiah writes that the Lord will make a new covenant with the people He is husband to: *"...After those days, saith the LORD, I will put my law in their inward parts, and write it in their hearts; and will be their God, and they shall be my people"* (Jer. 31:33).

Moses tells us in Deuteronomy that the word is in our mouth, in our mind, and in our heart so that we can obey the Lord, keep His commands, turn to Him with all our heart, live, and increase (multiply). However, if our heart turns away in disobedience and if we are drawn away to bow down and worship other gods, then we will certainly be destroyed. Just like the Israelites, we will not live long in the land we are supposed to enter and possess. Loving the Lord, listening to His voice, and holding fast to Him *is* choosing life (see Deut. 30:10-20).

If we are not listening to the voice of the Lord, we are not only bound to stray from our ordained place and position, but we are also likely to go astray in our thoughts. Throughout the Bible we are warned about the dangers of stinking thinking and encouraged to discipline ourselves to think on things that are lovely and pure, to have the mind of Christ, to put on the helmet of salvation, and so forth.[3] Because infection can spread if not treated, we need to use all the inward spiritual disciplines—prayer, meditation, fasting, and biblical studies—to keep our thoughts from running amok.

> **If you are not listening to the Lord's voice,
> your thoughts will likely go astray.**

One of the consequences of not holding fast to the Lord is that we stop listening to His voice and start listening to the voice of lust and pride. Listening to a toxic voice will, inevitably, lead to deficiencies in our own thinking, such as believing that the idols we serve will free or empower us. Our deficient thoughts may also fool us into thinking that our success is a product of our own intelligence, appearance, ability, or goodness. In addition, listening to diseased reasoning may dull our spiritual senses into thinking that we are smart enough, slick enough, or cool enough to avoid the consequences of self-centeredness. Perhaps we think that we know better than God does, so we engage in activities that are not good for us simply because they are available to us. When we succumb to the voice of pride and lust rather than listening to God's voice, we contract a STD!

When a STD is present, we can receive a word, but our diseased thinking prevents the seed from taking root in the center of our being where our knowledge of God's will resides. If our spiritual embryo is blocked by shallow thoughts and is, therefore, unable to embed itself in our spiritual womb where it can receive the necessary nourishment it needs to survive, our vision *will* die (see Luke 8:6; Matt. 13:5), and our destiny will perish.

LESSONS FROM JONAH AND DAVID

The prophet Jonah contracted a STD that almost killed him and the others around him. Jonah received a directive from God to go to Nineveh and preach repentance to its sin-ladened citizens. He received his instructions during an intimate moment with the Lord. However, instead of listening to the voice of God, he fled in the opposite direction, away from God's presence. Jonah's shallow, self-centered thinking landed him deep in the dank, dark, and disgusting belly of a whale. Trapped in desperation, Jonah would not be delivered from his dungeon until he repented for his disobedience and agreed to do what the Lord commanded. Throughout the story, Jonah had difficulty obeying God's order because he couldn't understand God's thoughts or God's ways. In fact, while listening to the voice of shallow thinking, Jonah's anger and frustration toward the Lord and the Ninevites continued to flourish rather than dissipate.

From a carnal, fleshly perspective, the prophet might have had a point; but from a spiritual perspective, his ideas were infected and diseased with self-centeredness (carnality) instead of God-centeredness (spirituality). Jonah could only see the current situation, but God could see the eternal. Our loving, heavenly Father was orchestrating a plan that seemed much too lofty for Jonah to wrap his mind around. The situation reminds me of how we struggle to understand that a disappointing or humiliating situation can work together for the good of us who love God and are called according to His purpose (see Rom. 8:28).

In the early chapters of his book, we see how Jonah's life and legacy as a preacher was in jeopardy. His promise was trapped in the wrong place. Wallowing in the belly of a whale, Jonah's potential was unable to thrive. Beloved, like Jonah, we must be careful that we do not allow Spiritually Transmitted Diseases, in the form of toxic thoughts, to create a tubal pregnancy and cause us to miscarry our destiny.

Likewise, David's promiscuous behavior, born out of impatience and restlessness, caused him to contract and transmit a STD. Sadly, this infection would claim the life of his beloved son as well as his incredibly brave and loyal ally. Though David had committed to serve God as His chosen king, this favored and celebrated warrior wandered away from the will of the Lord. In the eleventh chapter of Second Samuel, as we read about David's infidelity with Bathsheba, we find ourselves wondering, *What was he thinking?* After all, when this *chosen* and *anointed* king was supposed to go forth in battle, he lingered in the comfort of his palace. Instead of following God's direction, David found himself out of place and out of sorts. Accustomed to being on the front lines, he woke up in the middle of the night and strolled out onto his balcony. David could have and even *should* have fallen on his face before the Lord and prayed for the success of his men. If his thoughts were on the things of God, he very possibly would have slept peacefully through the night. Even if the Lord had awakened him, David could have received the direction, the correction, or even the comfort he was lacking that evening. Instead, impatient and restless, David centered his eyes, thoughts, and lust upon another man's wife.

Needless to say, David, the warrior king, did not choose his battle wisely when he chose to conquer Bathsheba rather than his nation's enemies. His understanding regarding his season as king, his pregnancy, his promise of greatness, and his purpose was clearly deficient and diseased. The murder of Bathsheba's husband, her pregnancy by the wrong person, and the subsequent death of their child represents, in the natural, what occurs in the spiritual. Deceit, chaos, and confusion ultimately lead to death and despair.

An examination of these Scriptures helps us comprehend the devastating effects that spiritual promiscuity can have on the seed of our destiny—our promise. If we are not diligent in fleeing youthful lusts, in growing in the knowledge of Christ, in loving and obeying Him, and in holding on to Him, we will end up wandering off, both physically and spiritually. We will not be steadfast and faithful in the ministry to which we are called. We will willingly let "whosoever will" pour into us. We will willingly listen to "whosoever will," as he or she speaks into our lives. We will willingly consent to "whosoever will," as he or she lies down with us. Just like the children of Israel and Bathsheba, we will run the risk of getting pregnant by the wrong person in the wrong place, and, ultimately, of experiencing a miscarriage—never bringing forth our promise.

Our medical correlation shows us that if a fetus isn't affixed in the womb, it can be miscarried. If you are going to maximize the potential of carrying out the healthy delivery of your promise, God's word must be affixed in your heart and in your mind (your spiritual womb). Then you trust what God has told you and what He has shown you. Even when it doesn't make sense, even if it looks like the promise is delayed or in danger of not coming to pass, trust that His word will not return unto Him void! In other words, God's word will accomplish whatever He designed it to accomplish (see Isa. 55:11).

God is so awesome that He protects the baby in a comfortable sac of amniotic fluid, which not only cushions the baby against blows to the mother's abdomen, but also provides easier fetal movement, promotes muscular and skeletal development, and protects the fetus from heat loss. However, the embryo has to bury itself well within the womb to gain the full protection of the uterus. Similarly, when we are exposed to the word of God, whether by reading it or by hearing it through the angelic messengers in our lives, we have to ensure that it is buried deep within our spiritual womb, for we know that the enemy will try to steal, kill, and destroy our word (see John 10:10). He will try to lead us to miscarry using trials and tribulations to steal our peace of mind and question our faith.

We must remember that, since the enemy has no power over our lives, he will try to use any means possible to convince us to doubt what God has said. After all, that's just what the father of lies did when he tried to persuade Eve that God lied when he told her that she and Adam would not die if they ate from the forbidden tree (see Gen. 3). Eve's thoughts became infected by a STD when she stopped listening to what God said and focused her attention on the physically attractive tree that was good for food and could make her wise.

Because the enemy has no power and God has all the power, the devil will also try to shift our focus off what we know in our hearts and in our minds. Some of the tools the enemy will try to use in order to cause us to abort or miscarry our destiny include: the lust of the flesh, the lust of the eyes, the pride of life, fear, and doubt. Therefore, it is risky business to go outside your covenant relationship with God.

Love Him with all your heart and all your soul. Listen to His voice. Lean not on your own understanding. Lean on the invincible Word of God. Hold fast to the Creator of the universe and the Lover of your soul. Then you will have life and increase. God sets life before you. The enemy offers death. Which will you choose?

I pray you will join me; I pray you will choose life!

ENDNOTES

1. See Deuteronomy 10:16; 11:18; Joshua 24:23; First Kings 8:61; Acts 28:27; and James 4:8.

2. For example, pelvic inflammatory disease, chlamydia, herpes, HIV-autoimmune deficiency, syphilis, gonorrhea, etc.

3. See Philippians 4:8; First Corinthians 2:16; and Isaiah 59:17.

CHAPTER 5

PREGNANT, WITH A WORD

And God remembered Rachel, and God hearkened
to her, and opened her womb (Genesis 30:22).

Not long ago, I was preparing to get away for some much needed vacation time. It wasn't that I just wanted to get away to relax or be revived. I wanted to be replenished. I knew that time away from my congregation would help generate new thoughts and innovative ways to help the ministry. I didn't know where God would lead me, but I expected something to be said and to happen, which, I knew, could only come from time spent nurturing my relationship with the Father.

At the beginning of my journey, I boarded a plane and settled into my seat in the first class cabin. Soon a flight attendant asked me if I would like something to drink. As she handed me my cup of water, I glanced around the cabin and noticed that the gentleman seated across the aisle, to my left, looked somewhat familiar. The attendant seemed to be making a fuss over him, as if he were someone of importance. Curious, I continued to look at him until I finally realized he was Don Shula, the famed football coach of the Miami Dolphins. As we were given our last instructions and taxied down the runway, he looked at me and said five profound words that I will never forget: "Are you ready for this?"

Isn't it amazing how God can speak only a few words and suddenly your life is changed? Isn't it amazing how God can immerse something so profound within your spirit that just a few words can connect with what's inside you and launch you deeper into your destiny? When Coach Shula asked me, "Are you ready for this?" it was as if God Himself was speaking directly to me, saying, "Get ready for your next level. Get ready to take off. Get ready to soar." I then became pregnant by a word from the Lord.

Think with me about being overshadowed by the Holy Ghost in the worship service. Though service is over and you have left the sanctuary, you are still lifted up in His presence. You cannot stop praising Him. You cannot stop crying. You may even still be speaking in other tongues. Excited by the inspiration and information you just received, it is as if a light bulb has been turned on in your spirit. You can't wait to get home to pray more, to read more, to praise more. You are on a spiritual high.

Before that service, you were just existing from day to day; you were walking with very little direction, yet walking nonetheless. You have been a consistent tither, a consistent prayer warrior, and a consistent praiser. Your attitude has been correctly open and receptive, yet before this service, you had not become pregnant. Then, at the precise moment that the word of the Lord came forth as your intended seed, destiny lodged inside your spiritual womb and you realized that you had finally conceived. Not knowing what the future holds, but knowing who holds the future, you are excited beyond words. You are ecstatic! You are inspired! You are pregnant!

By the time most women discover they are pregnant, they are already a few weeks along. Actually, the embryo is the size of a pinhead and is defined as a group of rapidly multiplying cells that don't initially resemble a baby. To start with, there are no outward signs of pregnancy. In the beginning, most women have a period of questioning before they know for sure if they are expecting. They may ask themselves, *Am I pregnant? Is it possible? What if I am pregnant?* Spiritually, we often have the same experience. We may know that we have heard a word from the Lord, but we still may question, *Have I actually received my word from God? Have I conceived?*

The experiences of three Bible matriarchs give us wonderful and powerful examples of how God will fill our spiritual wombs with the miracle of purpose and destiny. One of the things that truly amazes me about spiritual pregnancy is that it can happen even when we think time has passed us by. In the spirit realm, it doesn't matter how long it has been—if God said it, that settles it. Whatever *it* is (your dream, your purpose, your destiny), God *will* bring *it* to pass. Conception of purpose is the will of God for your life!

Let's examine three women who prayed to the Lord for a child. After hearing from God, each woman experienced a barren season, a time of being in the wilderness, a dry place, a season of longing for what the Lord had already spoken. After doing all they could do, to no avail, God stepped in and did what only *He* could do. *He* did exactly what *He* promised to do, and they conceived!

First, let us consider Sarah. Well before there were any signs of pregnancy, Almighty God proclaimed her to be the mother of many nations. Genesis 17:19 records this proclamation given to Abraham: *"And God said, Sarah thy wife shall bear thee a son indeed; and thou shalt call his name Isaac: and I will establish my covenant with him for an everlasting covenant, and with his seed after him."* Knowing what He had placed inside of them, God changed their names to reflect their destiny before they conceived. Abram's name was changed to Abraham (father of many), and Sarai's name was changed to Sarah (mother of many, and also lady or princess).

For several years following God's proclamation, Sarah remained without what she was called to bring forth. Frustrated by barrenness, Sarah tried to manipulate the situation and took matters into her own hands by coming up with her own answer to the question of how God was going to produce His promise. In spite of her interference, in the right season, and at the right time, God filled the womb of the person to whom He made the promise. Sarah conceived and became pregnant with God's word and promise.

Next, let us consider Rebekah. A prophetic word was also spoken over her life when she was called to be *"the mother of thousands of millions"* (Gen. 24:60). Rebekah married Isaac, the promised child of Sarah, who inherited the promise of Abraham. *"And Abraham gave all that he had unto Isaac"* (Gen. 25:5). Although Rebekah was barren, just like Sarah, *"the effectual fervent prayer of a righteous man availeth much"* (James 5:16b). The Bible says that Isaac prayed hard to God for his wife because his promise was also in her. Finally, because God's word accomplished what it is designed to accomplish (see Isa. 55:11), Isaac's prayer was answered and Rebekah's womb was filled with the promises of God.

Last, we will consider Rachel. For years, she was taunted by her sister, Leah, who bore many children to their husband, Jacob. It was through Jacob that God's promise to Abraham would continue, and it was Rachel whom Jacob chose to be his wife and bear his children. Yet, through a series of unforeseen events and deceit, Jacob married Leah. As Leah continually bore Jacob's children, Rachel, the chosen one, remained barren.

Like Rachel, how many of us have heard the call of God on our lives and received a word of destiny, yet watched other people get blessed and wondered, *Is God ever going to bless me?* Know this, beloved: God is not a respecter of persons; He is a respecter of principles. Rachel's story gives us hope because the Bible says in Genesis 30:22, *"And God remembered Rachel, and God hearkened to her, and opened her womb."* She conceived and became pregnant with God's promise.

In each woman's situation, God's proclamation was followed by an extended period of waiting and waiting and waiting. However, when the time was right, when the season was right, when the situation was right—*God did it!* In due time, God remembered their prayers; He remembered their loved ones' prayers; He remembered His own promised word; and then He opened their wombs.

> **Before you were formed, the Lord spoke destiny into your spirit.**

If you have been waiting and waiting and waiting, I am certain God has spoken a word into your life. Before you were formed in your mother's womb, the Lord spoke that word of destiny into your spirit. If you have been in time and in tune with God, as discussed in Chapter 3, then He will turn the barren situation around and allow you to conceive and bring forth what He has purposed in your life. God has opened your womb. Know that you are pregnant because He said He would do it. This is your season. Your dream will come forth. Never give up on God because prayer changes things! You *are* pregnant with a word! Be *"confident of this very thing, that he which hath begun a good work in you will perform it until the day of Jesus Christ"* (Phil. 1:6). He *will* bring it to pass! Nevertheless, you may still be asking, "How do I know I am pregnant?" In the physical and spiritual realms, confirmation of our condition provides a sense of relief in the process of pregnancy—or does it?

TESTING

But he knoweth the way that I take: when he hath tried me, I shall come forth as gold (Job 23:10).

Physically and spiritually, there is always a test to help us determine whether we have conceived. The testing process for pregnancy takes many forms. First, there is a physical examination performed by a doctor. Then there is a urine and blood test given for final confirmation. During the physical examination process, there is also a series of visual inspections, along with prodding and touching. Whatever the vehicle, there are two important things to note: 1) there is always a test, and 2) there are only two indicators, positive or negative (pregnant or not pregnant). Testing only exposes what is already there—or not there.

Similarly, in academic and professional settings, we will be tested. For example, students take tests so they and their professors can know whether they have adequately received the proper seeds of education and are ready to graduate. Testing also reveals in which areas the students need to improve. After testing has demonstrated that the students have retained the proper level of education, they will then be ready to apply what they have learned and move on to the next level.

The Greek definition of the word "test" means to examine, interpret, discern, discover, approve, prove, and demonstrate. Before we produce or ever bring forth what God has sown into us, we must be tested and examined. You must thoroughly understand that, because there is greatness in your belly, throughout your spiritual pregnancy a testing process will occur.

Physically and spiritually, there are signs of conception that can be seen by way of a visual examination. If you're like me, you grew up in an era when a visual inspection by a wise elder could reveal that a woman had conceived, even before she began to show outwardly. Supposedly, a particular vein in a woman's neck will pulsate, convincing an elderly mother that a woman is pregnant.

I will never forget the day that First Lady Martha Staples learned that we were pregnant. We had been praying for a child and had been trying to conceive for a few years. One day she came home and said, "Look at me. How do I look?" Of course I told her she looked beautiful, for she was a beautiful woman who had a Holy Ghost glow that would light up any room. Yet, it was not that glow to which she was referring. She wanted to know whether I saw what the elder had seen. She wanted to know whether I could see the signs of pregnancy. Even though she had not begun to show, to a keen eye, there were signs that destiny (our daughter Micah) had been conceived.

Let's revisit Mary, the mother of Jesus. As explained in the first chapter of Luke, verses 31-45, after Mary learned of her conception, she hastened to share her miraculous news with her cousin, Elizabeth, whom the angel told Mary was also experiencing a miraculous pregnancy. As soon as Elizabeth heard Mary's greeting, the Holy Ghost filled Elizabeth and told her that Mary was pregnant with the Lord. Actually, the infant resting in Elizabeth's womb was also filled with the Holy Ghost and leapt for joy at the first sound of Mary's voice. Mary didn't need to announce the miracle because her fellow servants in Christ (Elizabeth and John) were open to receiving the physical cues that announced Mary was pregnant with destiny—that she was pregnant with a word. In fact, Mary was not just pregnant with any word, she was pregnant with *the* Word of God (see John 1:1).

From this example, we can see that in order to successfully birth destiny, we need to fellowship with someone who believes in the impossible. Also, when we are pregnant with greatness, we will be better prepared to carry and deliver our promise if we can relate with someone who has been through a similar experience. It is incumbent upon us to find someone like Elizabeth—someone who is (relatively) close, someone who will honor what is inside us, someone who will believe simply because he or she has been there, too.

What's even more exciting when you are pregnant with destiny is that the Holy Ghost begins to examine you! God, the Chief Physician, begins to personally prod, touch, and examine you to determine whether you have received your seed. During this process, as you sense the eyes of the Lord upon you, you will begin to feel covered and protected. You will also notice a more intense spiritual pull to read the Word and an intense conviction if you try to go against the will of God concerning you and your seed of destiny. Though the examination process is not always comfortable, let it reassure you that you have, indeed, received your seed—that you are, indeed, pregnant with a word!

Spiritually, when we become pregnant and as God tests us, we start to emerge as pure gold. Job 23:10 reads, *"But he knoweth the way that I take: when he hath tried me, I shall come forth as gold."* And First Peter 4:12-13 states:

> *Beloved, think it not strange concerning the fiery trial which is to try you, as though some strange thing happened unto you: but rejoice, inasmuch as ye are partakers of Christ's sufferings; that, when his glory shall be revealed, ye may be glad also with exceeding joy.*

The bottom line is that we cannot bring forth unless we have been tried. We cannot bring forth unless we have been tested. We cannot safely deliver our destiny unless we have endured the test. Then we can know that we are prepared for what the next level has in store for us.

The greater the promise, the greater the test.

The trials that God uses to test our ability to bring forth His seed can vary in degree from assignment to assignment and from season to season. At this point, it is important that I share with you one critical point. *The greater the promise, the greater the test.* Do you remember the intense struggles Job had to overcome during his testing process? Though he lost everything during the testing of his faith, he successfully passed the test. As a result of his great endurance, he received double for his trouble! Similarly, though your examination process may be uncomfortable as you feel the pricks and prodding of the Holy Ghost, His glory, in the form of your destiny, shall be revealed with exceeding joy!

OVERJOYED!

> *But the angel said unto him, Fear not, Zacharias: for thy prayer is heard; and thy wife Elisabeth shall bear thee a son, and thou shalt call his name John. And thou shalt have joy and gladness; and many shall rejoice at his birth* (Luke 1:13-14).

Once you have conceived and learned that you are pregnant with destiny, you are overjoyed. Just like a man and woman who learn from their doctor that their efforts to become pregnant have succeeded, the announcement that "you are pregnant" with promise, destiny, and purpose brings great joy! The words, "you are going to have a baby," begin to resound in your heart.

Spiritually, you know that you are pregnant with a word because you feel the *unspeakable* joy that the Bible talks about! This joy is not given by the world and cannot be taken away! You know that you conceived because there is a fire that burns deep down inside, and when you think of His goodness, you practically burst! You know that when you went into worship, you entered in one way, but you came out another way. Not only do you know that, but others who know God and who have experienced spiritual pregnancy can also see it. There is something different in your prayer life. You have a burden for souls and a longing to tell everyone about Jesus. Your walk and your witness have changed, even if there is no evidence of the promise that is growing inside you.

Even before you see the symptoms, feel the movement, or hear the heartbeat, the mere knowledge that you are pregnant with a promise from God can produce a sense of extreme enthusiasm. The definition of the Latin word for "enthusiastic" is *entheos,* which means to be into God. In other words, when you are enthusiastic, you are into God. This is because God is into you. You are so filled with joy and so in tune to His presence that you can't stop the tears from flowing. As soon as you can, you call those closest to you and tell them about the announcement and confirmation of the wonderful word you received. Just like the new mother-to-be, you tell everyone who will listen that you are pregnant, and proudly announce that the Father of your child was none other than the Lord Himself!

Although many parents are overjoyed when they learn that they will bring a new life into the world, others are gripped with doubt and apprehension. However, in the spiritual realm, though we may be tempted to doubt our ability to conceive, it is important to positively receive the proclamation. Indeed, the higher the spiritual office, the more we are required to handle the word of God in a positive manner. We can see in the first chapter of Luke that Zacharias, the father of John the Baptist, helps illustrate this point. When he learned that his wife, Elizabeth, was pregnant, he was serving as a righteous priest in the temple of God. Though he faithfully lived a clean life of sincere service to his God, even into old age, his wife remained barren.

Then one day while performing his priestly duties of burning incense before the Lord and praying to Him, the Angel of the Lord appeared and announced that his and Elizabeth's prayers to have a child were finally being answered. Not only was Zacharias told that the Lord had miraculously answered their prayers, but he also was told that his seed would be great and would bring great joy and gladness to many. Unfortunately, Zacharias did not respond with great joy; nor was he overwhelmed by humble gratitude. Instead, Zacharias questioned the Lord. In response, the Lord took away his ability to speak until the child was born.

Those of us who know that our calling is a higher calling must understand the precept, "to whom much is given, much is required" (see Luke 12:48). Once we have done the work to position ourselves to hear from God, when we do hear Him, we must respond appropriately. The same spirit of gratitude that allowed for the conception must continue when we hear that God has answered our prayer.

Home pregnancy tests use the plus sign to indicate a positive result. Of all the symbols that could have been chosen to express pregnancy, it is interesting to note that the sign that represents addition and increase was chosen. If you are pregnant with a seed of academia, information has been added. If you are pregnant with *destiny*, then dreams, visions, and purpose have been added. Destiny requires walking worthily in the way that God wants you to walk. Because God has added life, your life has changed for the positive. The Bible says that Jesus came to give us life and that more abundantly (see John 10:10). God always adds to our lives, even in the testing process. Do not despise the process. The test is positive!

Congratulations, beloved, you have conceived. Embrace the process and bring forth your destiny!

CHAPTER 6

SICK IN THE MORNING

...weeping may endure for a night, but joy
cometh in the morning (Psalm 30:5).

Now that you are aware that you are pregnant, you will begin to experience the different phases of pregnancy—sometimes gracefully, and at other times awkwardly or irritably. Even if we have never had a baby, most of us have heard of the first, second, and third trimesters of pregnancy. During each stage of pregnancy, the baby grows and develops. Not only are there recognizable changes in the baby's development, but the mother's body begins to change, grow, and develop as well.

During the first trimester, in addition to the obvious weight gain and expansion of her belly, a woman may also feel light-headed, nauseated, and unusually tired. Her feet may begin to grow and swell; she may not be able to eat what she used to eat or do the things that she used to do. At times, she may become overly emotional and cry for any reason or for no reason at all. She may experience what has been termed in the natural as "morning sickness." Coincidentally, our flesh does the same thing when responding to the new life that is developing in our spiritual womb.

Before writing this chapter, I asked three women at the church about their morning sickness experiences. I wanted to find a good example of what might happen in the natural to gain insights into the typical sorts of things to expect when you are spiritually pregnant. As you will see, no two pregnancies are exactly the same. In fact, some of us will have extreme experiences, while most of us fall somewhere in the middle, between extreme and mild.

One young lady told me that she was sick twenty-four hours a day for three months. Another young lady told me she was unaware that she was pregnant. She stated that she thought the symptoms she was experiencing were caused by the flu. However, after several mornings of taking flu medication to no avail, she decided to consult her doctor. The results from her consultation concluded that she was not ill, but that she was going to have a baby.

The third young lady told me that when she shared the woes of her first trimester with others, they all professed to have answers to her ailments. She tried several of the methods suggested to her by well-meaning friends such as eating crackers or fruit in the morning. When she started telling me the story of the day she ate fruit before riding to the subway to work, I couldn't help but think that fruit, nausea, and riding a rocky train was a recipe for disaster. Indeed, she recounted that as the train started to move, she first got the dry heaves and then began to vomit. As soon as she started retching, others around her on the subway began moving out of the way to avoid the impending eruption. Thinking quickly, one gentleman pulled his newspaper out of its plastic bag. As soon as she got the bag, she started vomiting, while everyone else made haste of leaving her alone in that car of the train. Undoubtedly, she was sick in the morning. I am thankful to them for their "sick in the morning" experiences, since I do not have a physical "sick in the morning" story of my own.

Just as morning sickness is a sure sign of being physically pregnant, so it is with spiritual pregnancy. When we are pregnant spiritually, our spirit and our flesh react to the process, and we may also experience a type of spiritual "morning sickness." During this season, or trimester, of our spiritual journey, the joy of being pregnant should be apparent. However, we often experience confusion, doubt, nausea, and worry. Oftentimes, we may be so overwhelmed that our mornings may not be filled with any recognizable joy! For most of us, the great joy we initially experienced after an announcement of destiny suddenly departs, and our energy seems to be under the attack of an allergic reaction to the Alpha.

> **During this season, the seed and the word are expanding within your spirit.**

During this season, our spirits are being stretched to make room for the seed and the word that is expanding within us. This new heart and new spirit (see Ezek. 36:26) is growing against the grain of our normal behavior and pattern of thinking. Our body, mind, and spirit are responding to the changes caused by the seed that we have received into our lives. Once the dream has been conceived, our entire being begins to physically, emotionally, and spiritually react; our spiritual capacity is forced to expand, which nudges out our flesh and makes room for the gift.

As the DNA of greatness is nurtured in our spiritual wombs, it begins to grow and push against our former beliefs and self-perceptions. These spiritual genes guide the form and substance of our destiny and cause us to look and act like our Father. This development, however, is often accompanied by an uncertainty that can provoke misery, discomfort, and surges of "soul sickness." It may feel as if we are on a virtual emotional roller coaster until our spirits begin to adjust to the changes caused by the pregnancy.

When the Lord impregnates me with new plans, projects, revelations, directions, and assignments, I consistently experience symptoms of what I define as "spiritual morning sickness." I have noticed that during this phase of spiritual development, in addition to bouts with nausea, my diet often changes and my sleep is often disrupted. Sometimes, around two or three in the morning, I am abruptly awakened by the Holy Ghost. I must admit, during these seasons my body is tired, but my spirit is strong. Therefore, when I wake up, I am ready to hear what the Lord has to say.

At this stage in my ministry, as I listen for God and labor to carry a life-changing word (Sunday after Sunday, Wednesday after Wednesday); as I carry around in my belly a life-changing vision for the people of Southeast Washington, D.C. and its surrounding areas; as I carry the healing, direction, and elevation of 1,000 pastors from around the world in my womb; and as I carry out my assignment to establish apostolic authority in this region, it nauseates and irritates me to be around the pretenders of the gospel—those foolish ones who do not believe the Word of God.

As I walk out my destiny, it is unbearable to be with those who claim a depth of knowledge about God, but do not display the fruit of God in their lives. Spiritually, I find myself like many pregnant women in the first trimester: tired, irritable, and intolerant. I have no tolerance for those who proclaim a spiritual grandeur, but fail to do everything they can to position themselves so God can finish the work He has started in them. Even though I have experienced discomfort and complications, I hold on to the word in Psalm 138:8: *"The LORD will perfect that which concerneth me...."* After all, as believers, if you and I are going to birth God's plan in our lives, we must believe God's plan—even if it looks like He changed His mind. Not believing God is akin to someone who is pregnant, but whose inappropriate behaviors or inadequate preparations suggest he or she is denying the pregnancy.

> **If you are going to birth God's plan in your life, you must believe God's plan.**

Just as the symptoms of physical morning sickness vary from person to person, spiritual morning sickness also varies from saint to saint. However, I think it is safe to say that most of the symptoms will manifest during times of public worship. Maybe there was a time when you were the first to take off running for the Lord on Sunday morning, but now you find yourself barely making it to church. Or perhaps high praise and worship has started to annoy you, rather than fill you with joy. Instead of enjoying the mighty move of God as the saints begin to sing, dance, and shout, you may find yourself wishing others would "control" themselves and be quiet so that you can hear what the preacher has to say. Though you used to flow with the rhythm of the praises and reach for a rhyme or reason in the *rhema*, suddenly the worship experience is not as gratifying, soothing, or uplifting as it was before you conceived.

During the first trimester of your spiritual pregnancy, you may find yourself irritated and annoyed by every little thing that goes on around you. If you now find yourself struggling to praise, to worship, or to sow unto the Lord, then take a moment to stop and consider your condition. Maybe you are sick in the morning!

STRETCHING

Just as a pregnant woman's body must adjust and make room for the new life growing within her, so it is with the purpose that is growing in our spiritual wombs. Like the pregnant woman who has to change her eating habits, take prenatal vitamins, and get plenty of rest, a life-changing word from God will alter our behavior, thoughts, and actions. It *will* stretch us. For example, if we operate in insecurity, the genetic makeup of the seed of greatness will have to dominate and transform our insecure genes in order to produce an outcome that reflects the greatness that is now firmly attached to our core. Greatness and insecurity cannot dwell in the same womb.

As we accept that we are exactly who God says we are and that we can do exactly what He says we can do, a new identity begins to develop. All the while, as our new identity materializes and takes shape, our flesh accommodates our faith and makes room for the expansion of our rebirth. We need not be discouraged when this stretching process produces an uncomfortable feeling or attitude that fills our spirits with a lingering nausea. Rather, we should be encouraged—even if we cannot see exactly what God is doing; even if we have no idea how God is creating, forming, and developing a great destiny inside of us—because the queasiness we are experiencing is simply evidence that God is doing something wonderful in our spirits.

On any given day, a pregnant woman has no idea whether God is forming a brain cell, a toe, or hair follicle. All she knows is that a seed has been deposited, an embryo has been formed, and her baby is growing inside her. Through her season of morning sickness, God is working second by second, minute by minute, hour by hour, and day by day to transform her body, her attitude, her appetite, and her abilities. Likewise, our spirits, our attitudes, and our abilities need to be transformed and purged of what we should not carry with us to the next level of our spiritual destiny. Therefore, as God develops our blessing, He uses nausea to detach us from what we used to be. Like the pregnant woman whose system is purged of what she cannot tolerate, God transforms our spirits by causing us to purge our old nature. In fact, our attitudes, our appetites, and our abilities will change so drastically that we will no longer crave the things that we used to ingest.

The idea of spiritual morning sickness reminds me of the words to that old familiar gospel song by Anthony Tidwell entitled "I've Got a Testimony," which says:

> "As I look back over my life,
>
> and I think things over,
>
> I can truly say that I've been blessed,
>
> I've got a testimony.
>
> Sometimes I couldn't see my way through,

but the Lord He brought me out;

right now I'm free,

I've got the victory,

I've got a testimony."[1]

Though we won't see everything that is happening in our season of spiritual morning sickness, we can trust that God is truly blessing us. As we become who and what God wants us to be, we will be able to acknowledge that what we used to be, how we used to act, and how we used to talk will no longer sustain or satisfy us. As you and I progress along this journey of spiritual pregnancy, we must adhere to the direction penned by the apostle Paul in Romans 12:2, which says, *"And be not conformed to this world: but be ye transformed by the renewing of your mind...."* Then we will be able to analyze, approve, and attest to God's good, pleasing, and perfect will (see Rom. 12:2b). After our season of spiritual morning sickness has transformed our attitudes and our abilities, we will be able to deliver a truly triumphant testimony!

A WORD FROM GOD

A word from the Lord can also provoke dreams and visions or wake us up in the middle of the night. It can even keep us from continuing with some relationships that are unhealthy for our destiny. A word from God concerning our destiny can also turn our current daily routine upside down as it provokes us to step out into a new career, a new major in school, or a new level of finances. For example, if pregnant with a new career, aspiring professionals may find themselves working overtime and pushing past fatigue in order to get to the next level or promotion. Or, if pregnant with a new field of study, students may enroll themselves in evening classes and push past financial dilemmas in order to give birth to their destiny. A word from God can also unexpectedly interrupt our carefully crafted daily regimens and bring on a level of discomfort that is not always easy to adjust to or to readily identify.

As I write this book, I am embarking on yet another journey to build a house of worship for the people of God. I have been compelled by God to build the Tabernacle of Praise (a 4,000-seat sanctuary with overflow capacity, a state-of-the-art conference center, and classrooms) in the Washington, D.C., area. In this season in my ministry, not only do I feel the stretching, but also morning sickness currently is my constant companion. No longer am I being provoked to preach to a single denomination or bring forth a word for a particular denomination. No! God is yet stretching me to bring forth a word to people of varied faiths, races, and ideologies.

As God is stretching me to preach and minister to the saved and the unsaved, to the heterosexual and the homosexual, to the drug addict and the prostitute, and to the thief and the theologian, I am compelled to preach from a worldwide view. The Lord has given me a "whosoever will, let them come" word (see Rev. 22:17). This is not a biased word or an exclusive word. Rather, it is a *"God so loved the world"* word (John 3:16). In other words, I have been assigned to fish, but not just with one fishing pole. Rather, I have been launched out into the deep places, as instructed by His word. The Lord has shown me that if I throw a net that is large enough, God will catch whomever *He* wants to catch. All I have to do is preach His Word to the lost and to the saved.

As I moved from preaching two services on Sunday morning to three services at the Temple of Praise (our current 2,500-seat sanctuary with 500 overflow capacity), I felt the stretch and saw the stretch marks forming. As I reflect on the stretch marks I received during my last pregnancy (building our church at its current location), which are still so fresh in my mind that I cannot overlook them, I cannot help but feel that, with this pregnancy, I am being stretched more than ever before. As the Lord leads me through this Kingdom assignment, I ponder what I will look like, how misshapen I will become, and how marred I will be. He is beginning to stretch my form and fashion me beyond recognition. All the while, I know that He is shaping me and making me to be more like Him. For as the Bible says in First John 3:2:

> *Beloved, now are we the sons of God, and it doth not yet appear what we shall be: but we know that, when he shall appear, we shall be like him; for we shall see him as he is.*

Don't forget, beloved, that *stretching* to increase your ability to become a carrier of God's redemption plan and *spiritual morning sickness* are both part of the same process! You may find yourself having to praise God without the happiness to which you have been accustomed or which used to automatically fuel your excitement to praise. During this phase of your pregnancy, you may even have to force yourself to praise. That, too, is part of the spiritual reproduction process!

As you struggle to give God all the praise and all the glory, it will be helpful for you to try to imagine how King David felt when he wrote, *"I shall yet praise him."*[2] In spite of how sick you get during the first trimester, you must acknowledge the miraculous event taking place inside your being and continue to praise God from whom all blessings flow. Your praise, which was once spontaneous, may become sacrificially based on what you know to be true in spite of the facts of your circumstances.

If we are not careful during this glorious impartation, the emotional ups and downs of this season may cause us to think that we have merely caught the flu or some other temporary ailment as a result of being exposed to folks who were sick. Or we may suppose we are suffering with another kind of physical, mental, or emotional illness. If the symptoms of our pregnancy do not mimic the symptoms we have observed by watching others go through this process, we may simply be blinded from the evidence or ignore the clues that reveal we are expecting. However, let me assure you that we *are pregnant* and are simply reacting spiritually to what God is doing for us, in us, and through us.

BE CAREFUL

Since it is difficult to fully understand what is happening in the spiritual realm during the first trimester of our spiritual pregnancy, we must be very careful whom we allow into our lives and whom we let pour into or minister to our spirits. When overshadowed by the Holy Spirit and impregnated with a gift from God, we must not allow anyone to misdiagnose us.

When we learn we are pregnant with destiny and begin to go through a season of spiritual morning sickness, it is imperative that we find seasoned saints who have previously gone through this process and successfully delivered their promise. We must find a saint whose past experience allows him or her to correctly diagnose our symptoms without exposing us to anything that might cause us to prematurely birth or miscarry the greatness God has placed within us. Like a mother who has already given birth, our seasoned saint must know how to maneuver through the first trimester and be able to teach us what to eat in order to make it through our season of morning sickness.

Though we may be tempted, we cannot let the ill effects of morning sickness stop us. We still have to keep moving, we still have to continue working, and we still have to take care of our families. Even though you may not want to go to church, and even though you may not want to partake in the Word of God, you must press on. You must not let morning sickness stop you. When you are in this weakened state, you need someone who will tell you, "Baby, you have to eat something!" "Come on! Let's go to church!" "Let's read the Word!" "Let's give God the glory!" If you do not have someone of like or greater maturity to guide you through your first trimester of spiritual pregnancy, you run the risk of miscarriage.

> **During spiritual pregnancy, increase your daily devotion, worship, and study time with God.**

Most doctors counsel expectant mothers to increase their meals from three medium-portioned meals a day to six small portions of food throughout the day. During our spiritual pregnancy, we must also increase our daily devotion, worship, and study time with God—particularly in the first trimester of destiny. During this season, increasing our Word consumption will cause us to gain more knowledge as well as wisdom.

If you picked up this book and have recently been experiencing these symptoms, more than likely you are pregnant with destiny. Your spirit is making room; it is getting you ready to carry and soon deliver your destiny. The pain will not last forever. The morning sickness will subside. The unexpected tears will cease. The confusion will turn into direction, for God is not the author of confusion. Joy will come! The confusion and doubt will dissipate. What you have been experiencing is just the early signs of destiny growing and developing inside you. God is getting ready to hand over your miracle! Get ready to bring forth your destiny! Take comfort in the great men and women of God who have gone through this season before you—you are not alone!

Unfortunately, the flesh usually resists change. This is why Paul wrote about the two laws with which he wrestled—the flesh and the spirit (see Gal. 5:16). It's our flesh that is resisting our new seed of purpose. When we find ourselves backsliding or doing something that is in opposition to the doctor's orders concerning the maintenance of a healthy pregnancy, we must keep in mind that our flesh (carnal self) is trying to come against the promise. For example, if a woman eats too much when she is pregnant, she may suffer a significant level of discomfort. Similarly, if we try to kick against the "pricks" when we are pregnant with promise, our bodies will react (see Acts 26:14). We may be sick in the morning, uncomfortable in the afternoon, and unable to sleep at night, but this too shall pass.

The key to getting through this experience is to remember that flesh initially appears to reject the conception, but ultimately makes room for and prepares a way for the gift. Just as a female's body was designed by God to carry a baby full term, in like manner, our flesh was designed to make room for the seed, despite the false sense of resistance. God knew us before we were formed in our mothers' wombs. Similarly, He knows our destinies. He knew, before we were born, which of us would become doctors, lawyers, preachers, teachers, and scientists. He has already designed and made us to be capable of carrying and bringing forth His great purpose for our lives!

Get ready, my brother or sister, because if you are saved and filled with the Holy Ghost, then you and your flesh are subject to the Spirit of God. You and your flesh must make way for the gift and submit to the authority of the promise and destiny lying therein. If God said it, that settles it! Take a moment—put down this book and say, "I submit, Lord! I submit!"

ENDNOTES

1. "I've Got a Testimony," lyrics by Anthony Tidwell, performed by Rev. Clay Evans & The AARC Mass Choir, © 1995 Meek Records.

2. See Psalm 42:5,11 and 43:5.

CHAPTER 7

DESTINY DISTRACTIONS

*Now it came to pass, as they went, that he entered
into a certain village: and a certain woman named
Martha received him into her house. And she had a
sister called Mary, which also sat at Jesus' feet, and
heard his word. But Martha was cumbered about
much serving, and came to him, and said, Lord, dost
thou not care that my sister hath left me to serve alone?
bid her therefore that she help me. And Jesus answered
and said unto her, Martha, Martha, thou art careful
and troubled about many things: but one thing is
needful: and Mary hath chosen that good part, which
shall not be taken away from her* (Luke 10:38-42).

Once a woman learns she is pregnant, it is important for her
to adopt and maintain a proper eating regimen. During pregnancy, eating the right fruits, vegetables, and foods low in sodium,

coupled with monitoring her sugar intake, is extremely important. Ingesting the proper amounts of protein, folic acid, and other vitamins is also critical. Keep in mind that while a woman is pregnant, she is not eating for herself alone; the fetus also gets nourishment from the mother. The focus on nutrition may be easier at the start of the second trimester, especially for those women whose first trimester is agitated by morning sickness or who take longer to adjust to the idea that they are having a baby.

Similar to the roles of exercise and weight control, diet is also crucial to experiencing a healthy pregnancy and delivering a healthy baby. If not diligent, a pregnant woman may become distracted by the rise and fall of her emotions, energy level, or appetite. If she does not remain focused, the expectant mother may deviate from the instructions and dietary plan ordered by her physician. In fact, there are many occurrences that take place during this phase of the pregnancy that can distract either parent from celebrating and preparing for the miracle of life. Changes in physical appearance and the ability to function as usual can also disturb either one or both of the parents, especially if the changes lead to worries about unattractiveness or if they disrupt the intimate sexual union between the couple. Other preoccupations such as worries about labor, delivery, motherhood, fatherhood, or financial difficulties may also plague the expecting parents.

The word "distracted" means to worry, to twist; to be drawn here and there, diverted, sidetracked, troubled, confused, or anxious. Oftentimes, we believers can become distracted when we look for alternative answers to our questions, substitute solutions for our concerns, or interchangeable instructions for our lives. In turn, this self-found information can, either directly or indirectly, serve as a distraction that keeps us from accepting the guidance of the Holy Spirit who has been assigned to teach and comfort us.

Spiritual distractions come in a variety of forms. Some individuals are tempted to read their horoscope to find a word based on the sign of the times under which they were born, while others attempt to find a word through a psychic reading. However, placing one's faith in horoscopes or psychic readings can open our spirits up to difficulties in conceiving or in successfully nurturing our destiny until the appointed time of delivery. In addition, feasting on foolishness, gossip, and faultfinding will surely distract us and limit our ability to focus on what is right and true. Obsessing about life's circumstances and succumbing to feelings of anxiety and fear over areas that we can't control will also distract us.

As Luke 10:38-42 suggests, Martha was distracted with much serving. In her home sat the Savior of the world. Nevertheless, her concern was more about entertaining Christ and running her household, than it was about gleaning from the Teacher, Master, Rabbi, the Living Word who was in her midst. Instead of asking the Lord what direction she should take, Martha was so encumbered by what Mary was not doing that she ordered the Lord to do what *she* (Martha) wanted Him to do. Oh, how often do life's distractions shift our attention away from the gift that is dwelling within our belly and away from the Father of our destiny as He moves to give us His time, His love, His direction, and His guidance?

If we are pregnant with promise, we must be sure that we are getting the proper nourishment from the Word and are paying close attention to all that God has commanded—turning not from it to the right or to the left (see Josh. 1:7-8). As we carry the seed of promise deep within our spiritual wombs, we must also stay focused as we go through the ups and downs life has to offer.

NO WAYS TIRED—FOOD FOR THE JOURNEY

Galatians 6:9 tells us that we must not get weary in doing the right things. Even though we know that greatness lies within us, we must also understand that we will still face great challenges that may make us want to quit. I have learned firsthand that the greater the vision, the greater the anointing; and the greater the anointing, the greater the trial.

> **Even though greatness lies within, you will still face challenges that may make you want to quit.**

Jesus provided the perfect illustration for this principle. In order to reign and fulfill His purpose, He had to die. In fact, His prayer in the garden of Gethsemane lets us know that He would have preferred different instructions from His Father (see Matt. 26:39). Nevertheless, Jesus chose to lay down His life because He knew this was the only way we could be reconciled to God. Though Jesus could have brought an end to God's plan for redemption at anytime before or during His crucifixion experience, He did not. Instead, He remained focused on God's word and plan. The rest, dear saint, is history.

One of my greatest trials while pregnant with a great promise started out simple enough; however, it quickly spiraled into a potentially massive distraction. While shaving one morning, I noticed a small bump on the right side of my neck between my earlobe and my jawline. I figured it was harmless and would soon go away. Unfortunately, over the next few weeks that little bump grew at an alarming rate, so I decided to have my doctor take a look at it.

I will never forget his diagnosis. It was cancer. It was a line of demarcation in my life. It was a season of trial, tribulation, pruning, and developing. It was a quantum leap from mediocrity to greatness.

Looking back on that day, I remember the urgent awareness that I needed to pray. As always, God kept me during this dark diagnosis. With heightened awareness, I listened as the doctor explained that there was a tumor in my salivary gland and that it showed much inconsistency, which meant it was both benign and malignant. Since malignant cancers often spread, he wanted to immediately schedule me for surgery; however, he warned that the surgical team would have to cut the nerves that operate the muscles on that side of my face. This meant that, in all likelihood, my face would droop and my speech would be severely impaired.

Needless to say that was not what a man called to preach the gospel wanted to hear. Not only was I in a battle for my life, but I was also in a battle for my divine destiny. Having no other choice but to trust God, I agreed to the let the surgical team remove the threatening tumor.

As I faced the darkness of uncertainty, on the day of my surgery I noticed that the sun outside was shining brightly. It was a truly beautiful day. Following my operation, my doctor walked into my room and asked, "Reverend Staples, how are you doing?"

"I'm fine," I answered.

Oddly enough, my doctor turned and walked out of my room. In a clipped and excited tone, I overheard him speaking to someone in the hall. "He's talking pretty plain. He's talking. I don't understand it. He's talking!"

Then he and the neurosurgeon walked into my room, each looking quite astonished. The neurosurgeon's next words explained their amazement. "We thought your speech would be slurred because we cut the nerves in your face that affect your muscles." He then went on to explain, "Your face should be drooping because there are no muscles. There are no nerves to hold the muscles." He then held out his left arm, grabbed his elbow with his right hand, and pumped his left arm up and down, while he continued to explain, "Because you see, when we do this [his arm moving up and down] and we move our arm, that's all done by nerves, which are attached to our muscles." Then he remarked, "There's nothing to hold your face up. We don't understand why your face is not drooping and has not fallen."

Remembering that it was a beautiful day outside, I looked at both of my doctors and said, "If you go outside, you can look up at the sun. The same power that's holding up the sun is holding up my face." And, that's been my testimony all these years. You see, though the surgery severed the nerves that controlled my speech, though I had a painful road of recovery ahead of me, though I would be left with a noticeable scar running along my neck, I did not let any of that stop me from giving God the glory.

Even with the recognition that God had miraculously spared my life and my speech, I was not completely healed. The right side of my face was frozen. It would not move. As a matter of fact, my eye would not close. It stayed open all of the time. I could not even blink. To protect my eye, I wore tinted glasses and often an eye patch to bed at night.

In addition, I soon learned that, when I read out loud or tried to preach, there were certain words I couldn't pronounce. For example, the word "professor" came out sounding like "fafessor." If

I was in the middle of a sermon, it would distract me, and I would think, "Oh, God, I can't pronounce this word."

Though I knew I was an actual miracle through whom God revealed His healing grace, I still had to endure the difficult physical and emotional consequences of my circumstances. As a result of my affliction, I became distracted with an enormous amount of self-doubt. With all that I was up against, I needed to decide whether or not I would climb up out of my pit of despair and continue to preach.

Yes, I was and am very thankful to God for healing me and removing the cancer; however, I still had to walk through the valley of distraction caused by cancer's painful aftereffects. If I had succumbed to the intended distractions as they invaded my life, I may have miscarried my destiny. Thankfully I have since come to realize that the pain, the scarring, and the changes in my speech were all part of my maturity process.

After the surgery, in order to get my muscles to respond, I underwent an extensive therapy regime. This involved the uncomfortable process of placing electrodes on my face and zapping me with painful volts of electricity designed to stimulate the nerves, so I could finally close my eye and speak more clearly.

I endured the repeated and painful shocks to my face two or three times a week for more than a year, with no major improvement. Finally I decided that I had had enough. Seeing no reason to continue the electrifying torture, I abandoned my therapy treatments.

Of course, I continued to ask the Lord to heal me. By that point, I was seriously concerned whether or not I could continue to preach effectively. Not only did I want my sermons to contain strong substance, I also wanted my words to be clear. So, though

I didn't quit preaching, I went through a period where I didn't accept many major preaching engagements.

The only thing that kept me going was the word God had placed within my belly that I was destined to become a great preacher. A few weeks after I quit going to therapy, I pleaded, "Lord, You gotta do something. Heal me. Do something!" Praise God, after that desperate prayer, the Lord healed me. After a year of pain with no gain, after a season of doubt and shame, I was finally able to move my face. Not only could I close my eye, but I also could wink. Not only could I move my jaw, but I also could talk just as plainly as I talk today.

It is important to note that, in spite of my embarrassing speech impediment, I knew I needed to remain faithful to God's assignment. If I was going to fulfill God's purpose, I had to embrace His plan. I had to stay focused, steadfast, and unmovable as I continued to abound in the work of the Lord. Even though everything around me suggested the contrary, I could not afford to forget that the Lord had spoken a word over my life and instructed me to preach the gospel.

When we find ourselves pregnant with promise, purpose, and destiny, we need a solid, life-sustaining word from God. We need a word that will nourish and strengthen us so that we can go the distance, despite the internal and external destiny distractions that weigh heavily upon our spirits. Without a solid, life-sustaining word, distraction will doom our destiny to destruction.

Hebrews 5 and 6 provide an excellent illustration that directly relates to our need for proper nourishment from God's Word during such difficult times. Here, the author of Hebrews uses "milk" and "solid food" figuratively, contrasting basic and advanced instruction as a requirement for growing in the knowledge of the Word of

God. As we mature and destiny is firmly established in our wombs, it is critical to examine what we eat in order to properly nourish our word of destiny. We must be careful that we do not to allow the enemy to distract us from doing the necessary things that allow us to successfully accomplish our God-given purpose and plan.

In addition to the example of Abraham as described in Hebrews chapter 6, the Bible is replete with those who sought the meat of the Word in order to produce the destiny created within their spirits. Moses went to the mountains to obtain the meat of the Word from the Almighty concerning His commission and instructions for Israel's freedom. Before Samuel was released as a prophet to the kings of Israel, he spent his childhood living in the temple and assisting the priests in their worship of the Lord. And, of course, we can't forget how Mary sought meat when she traveled to sit at the feet of the more mature Elizabeth in order to be fed, nurtured, and sustained until it was time to reveal the God in her—the Word of God made flesh.

> **For a successful delivery, you need
> the sustenance of the Word.**

In the same way that a protein-rich diet promotes the delivery of a healthy baby, a mature word promotes the mental and physical stamina needed for the successful delivery of our God-given promise. A watered-down or milky word is simply not substantial enough for the second and third trimesters of a spiritual pregnancy. Therefore, if we expect a successful delivery, we need the sustenance provided by the meat of the Word. Now that we are eating for two, we must ensure that what has been imparted into our spirits is nourished by scripturally sound principles. Otherwise, our destiny cannot properly grow and mature. When bombarded by distractions, we do not need a milk message; we need a message rich in meat. Milk diets are for babies, *not* for baby carriers!

Small-minded messages tend to exhaust our energy, pollute our passion, and sadden our spirit. Consequently, during my season of suffering, I learned that talking or preaching on a superficial or shallow level left me in a vulnerable position. You can be sure that a milk diet will also weaken you and cause you to waver. Therefore, in order to avoid entertaining messages that are not consistent with God's Word, you must carefully choose your dining options as well as your dining partners. Simply put, when you are pregnant and carrying purpose, you do not have time to talk to anyone who has given up. You cannot entertain anyone who blames others for not reaching his or her goal. You cannot converse with anyone who says there is any way other than God's way. Now that you know exactly what God has said, you must be sold out to the vision, the purpose, the destiny that He has given you. To avoid a devastating miscarriage, you cannot afford to let anything distract you from your purpose.

While dealing with the aftermath of the healing, the scar left behind by my surgery taught me that God will often leave behind something to constantly remind us that *He* is the one who heals. Ultimately I came to realize that even if we, like Jacob in Genesis 32, are left with a limp—or a scar or stretch marks—that we did not have before, we will become better than we used to be. I fought my destiny distractions for three months before I was able to physically see that my pronunciation was improving. Nevertheless, in order to produce God's offspring, I had to go through the ridicule of being laughed at behind my back.

Even when I wondered if God would do what He said He would, it was crucial that I continued to speak the principles and follow the precepts God taught me in order to walk in victory. Since tough times call for a tough word, I had to remain strong in the Lord. Therefore, I needed to consistently ingest God's protein-rich, power-packed Word with gladness. It was His Word, and only His Word, that sustained me so that I could progress through the labor process and deliver my destiny.

WALKING BY FAITH, NOT BY FEELINGS

Since we are now showing and are obviously pregnant, it is evident that we are being prepared for a great work. However, we must also be careful not to draw unnecessary attention to ourselves or do things to win the affection of others. When things get a little rough, our flesh tends to seek compassion. When things do not move as fast as we would like, we may become tempted to look for other ways to satisfy our ambitions or desires. Like the pregnant woman who wants ice cream and cookies to soothe her cravings, we may want sugar-coated advice and direction. We might want someone to rub our spiritual feet to satisfy our emotional peaks and valleys. However, as we know, too much sugar during pregnancy can cause the dangerous condition called gestational diabetes. Therefore, we must avoid sugar-coated advice or a kindergarten word. The fact that you are pregnant means you are of the age to become pregnant. Consequently, whatever you ingest must be consistent with your condition.

I can imagine, as new symptoms or difficulties arise, some first-time moms-to-be may be tempted to frequently call their doctors to gain additional instructions or guidance. They might even start to question their doctor's knowledge or interest if their questions or concerns seem to be downplayed or ignored. Therefore, I should warn you, in the midst of your pregnancy and during the season of distraction, know that there will be times when you don't hear from God. You can, however, trust Him when you cannot trace Him. Just as Jesus had to endure His Friday and Saturday night in the grave in order to obtain resurrection power, we too must endure our grave experience. We too must die to ourselves, our fears, and our personal concerns. We too must allow God to raise us out of our grave and into our destiny. If we remain focused and rebuke the distractions during a silent period, the meat of the Word will sustain us.

In order to survive the potentially distracting silence and struggle of my healing season, I held on to the power-packed meat messages provided by the Word. Ultimately, God *did* speak! He told me to move to D.C. In the same year as my surgery, during the healing process, I had a vision from God regarding the church that I would eventually pastor. This experience taught me that, in order to get what God had for me, I needed to endure a period of testing when I could have easily given up.

Likewise, when you are carrying great purpose in your belly, you must persevere to remain focused. Therefore, it is helpful to be aware that being pregnant with destiny is like walking a tightrope; you cannot look to the left or to the right. You must operate like a horse with blinders on. When the enemy tries to use naysayers to distract you, a milky or watered-down word won't help you. You need more than just a new member's class. Along with spending quality time in prayer with the Scriptures, you need a prophetic word, as well as a *rhema*.

No matter the tactic, we must not submit to the adversary's attempts to delay or deny us from reaching our destiny, *even* if there appears to be an easier way. Since distractions can be slight and subtle, if we are to achieve God's tailor-made purpose for our lives, then we must remain focused on what God has told us and follow His exact instructions.

We need only examine the life of Abraham to fully understand what can happen to our promise if we get distracted by an easier way. In Genesis 15:4, God told Abram that He would give him an heir from his own body, yet Abram did not follow the Lord's instructions to deliver the promise. Like the pregnant woman who shuns her doctor's orders and decides to have ice cream in the middle of the night, Abram also became distracted and took Hagar, his wife's handmaiden, in order to have a child. What was birthed from the distraction was not the promise. Rather, Hagar gave birth to Ishmael (the product of Abram's impatience), not Isaac (the product of God's promise).

In order to avoid being distracted and birthing something other than what God has intended, we should stay alert for an *instructional* word to believe in; a word like that spoken by the prophet Isaiah when he instructed the Israelites to keep their faces like flint (see Isa. 50:6-8). In addition, praising God is another wonderful way to increase our life-sustaining faith. Therefore, we need a resounding word of praise, such as the one King David used to encourage himself as he sang, *"I will bless the LORD at all times: his praise shall continually be in my mouth"* (Ps. 34:1).

By spending your days praising the Lord, you will avoid trying to talk your way out of your test. This will also make it difficult for folks to fill your mind and spirit with depressing or frightening messages. Therefore, take to heart the Scripture, *"Let the words of my mouth, and the mediation of my heart, be acceptable in thy sight..."* (Ps. 19:14). Know that if you can keep a careful watch over what you say and what you do, you will keep the enemy from gaining a foothold in your spiritual pregnancy. Then the enemy of your destiny will see that he cannot intimidate you or batter you with the fear of failure or the temptation to give up.

> **Keep careful watch over what you say and do.**

As we progress further into the latter trimesters of our spiritual pregnancy, we may find that we are both physically and spiritually more tired than we were before we became pregnant with a word. As we fight fatigue, it is easy to become discouraged by distracting comments and questions and advice such as, "You haven't had that baby yet? How much weight have you gained? Child, take the epidural. I was in labor for twenty-eight hours. I had a C-section; there was no way I was going through all that pain. Since you're over forty, does your doctor think the baby will be ill?"

Receiving a righteous word in this phase of your pregnancy makes you keener, sharper, and more astute. Just as new parents read and research successful child-rearing techniques, destiny carriers should also seek out the underlying principles and universal truths that will best serve them throughout their ministry. Let me help you start your parenting strategy notebook by sharing with you what I have learned. In spite of how it looks, everything *will* turn out all right; your nighttime weeping *will* turn into morning leaping; and, if you search through your own faith files that document your history with God, you will soon conclude that your heavenly Father is *always* in control and is *always* faithful to His word!

A FINAL WORD

As pregnant saints, we need to hear a message that is relative to our situation. We need to follow doctor's orders. We need to be consistent in our walk with Christ and our attendance at church. We must remain faithful to the ministry that releases seed capable of seeping into our talents, infiltrating our gifts, permeating our thoughts, and invading our dreams. We must immerse ourselves in the Word.

Instructions about proper nutrition during pregnancy have to be tailor-made to the individual. This requires a doctor to review the patient's medical records, which includes his or her past and present physical and psychological health status. In most cases, the doctor will also be able to assess future health conditions and to predict life outcomes. The corresponding lesson for those of us who carry destiny in our wombs is that we must have a covering who will know what and when to feed us during each phase of our spiritual pregnancy. For you, that will be your pastor or shepherd. He or she will know what word is good for you and what contains too much salt, not enough protein, or too much sugar. Unlike someone unfamiliar with you and your condition, your covering will invest in the healthy delivery of your promise.

Think about it for a moment. Would a pregnant woman needlessly change doctors for prenatal care in the middle of her pregnancy? Of course not—a doctor who is unfamiliar with a patient's medical history runs the risk of making the wrong diagnosis, prescribing the wrong medication, and giving the wrong medical instructions. So it is with our spiritual condition. Changing pastors and churches in the midst of our pregnancy can put our pregnancy at risk. Although a new pastor is preaching the word of

God, that word may not be what we need for our season. Another pastor, one not familiar with us or our spiritual history, may feed us something that causes us to miscarry.

> Changing pastors and churches
> during your spiritual pregnancy
> can put that pregnancy at risk.

There are times during our pregnancy when we need firm direction, correction, and even reproof in order to deliver safely. Just like the pregnant woman who is prescribed bed rest, sometimes we have to remain at our home church to get what we need for a successful delivery. While we are pregnant, we must be careful not to look for a passive or sweet version of the gospel.

CHAPTER 8

ULTRASOUND

There came a sound... (Acts 2:2).

Every mother-to-be receives a routine ultrasound during the second trimester of her pregnancy. Also called a sonogram, this diagnostic tool uses high-frequency sound waves to produce internal images of the human body. Some of the images produced by an ultrasound include the unborn child's head, legs, feet, arms, hands, profile, and internal organs. In addition, it can even show the baby's heartbeat, as well as other body movement, often before the mother senses the slightest flutter within her womb. I especially appreciate the ultrasound as a primary source of information regarding what parents can expect in the coming weeks and months. As discussed in the previous chapter, knowledge and understanding help focus our energy on the choices we need to make rather than on worrying about what we cannot control.

I must admit I am in awe of the physics that lead to the creation of a visual image through the use of sound. I do not pretend to fully understand the mechanics involved, but the basic idea is as follows: sound waves travel into the body, reflect changes in density, then return to the scanner where the sound is transformed into an image. This specialized use of sound waves allows physicians to determine the location, size, condition, and viability of the fetus. Consequently, the ultrasound allows for a more accurate prediction of the delivery date and can even be used to determine the sex of the baby.

As you experience the changes associated with the growth of your spiritual fetus, there will come a time when you will also be able to receive an image of what is taking place within you. When this happens, sound must travel from the Creator (God the Father) through the scanner of the Holy Spirit to search your inner being (your heart, mind, and soul) in order to come into contact with, and illuminate, the new, denser substance developing deep within your core.

When the sound wave encounters a new organism with a different density, such as a fertilized egg, part of the sound wave is reflected back as an echo. When the Holy Spirit transmits the sound, which reveals the changes occurring deep within you, it rests on you, fills you (see Acts 2:2), and testifies (echoes) to your spirit that, as God's heir, you possess the promise and share in His glory (see Rom. 8:16-17). Now, *that* is good news!

Next the echo is sent back to the Father who processes and transforms it into the image of Christ so that it can be witnessed by those who have eyes to see. Once we tap into the knowledge, the Holy Ghost helps us monitor the growth, size, and health of our destiny so that we can properly attend to any defects and minimize any risks that threaten the healthy development and delivery of our destiny.

Like millions of expectant parents who have run to a doctor's office to see the first picture of their unborn child via an ultrasound examination, it is only natural that, once the Spirit of God has overshadowed us, we too long to know what we are carrying, when we will give birth, and what our destiny looks like. Therefore, if we expect to access the things of God and understand what He has called us to do in regard to our divine destiny and our purpose, we will also need to receive a spiritual ultrasound and obtain a picture of what God has in store for us.

However, just as a physician does not use an ultrasound to merely satisfy a parent's curiosity, spiritual ultrasounds also have a more important purpose. To ensure the best outcome for our destiny, we must not use the information we receive from our spiritual ultrasound to merely monitor the image of our destiny. We should also use it to monitor the health of our heavenly blessing, pray against spiritual destiny defects, and seek to discover whether our baby (destiny) is properly positioned for a healthy and safe delivery.

> **You need to receive a spiritual ultrasound to see what God has in store for you.**

THE FIRST GLIMPSE

The first picture, or spiritual sonogram, of our promise may take the form of a prophecy spoken over our lives or a divine revelation in our spirits. Whatever the form, it is sure to excite us and ignite a passion to prepare for what is rapidly growing within our inner being. Our first ultrasound also makes the promise more tangible and provides us with a greater knowledge and understanding of our destiny and how we should proceed.

Once you have received this first glimpse, you may venture to give your promise a name. For example, you may say, "When I start my construction company, I'm going to name it 'John's Construction' after my grandfather." Or, "When I open my beauty shop, I'll name it 'Mary's Marvelous Manes' in memory of my mother who passed before she could see my dream manifest." Whatever name you choose, as most parents who have just obtained a first glance at the manifestation of their seed, the excitement and anticipation are rapidly growing.

I often marvel at the way God takes individuals born in poverty or addicted to drugs and exposes them to a picture of their possibilities. It gives me great joy to watch these dear saints being set free to achieve great things in God. In fact, it never ceases to amaze me when I watch someone's crazy faith grow in proportion to his or her increasing knowledge of Christ. If you have ever been pregnant, you are well aware how difficult it is to try and explain to someone what the blurry image depicts. You understand that no one sees it as clearly as you. Though you try to describe what you see and feel, no one can really understand it as you do.

> **Don't be discouraged when others
> cannot see what God has for you.**

Don't be discouraged, beloved, when others cannot see what God has for you. The reason they are unable to see it is because He has not shown it to them. They weren't at the office when the doctor (God) helped you make out the details of the vision. In addition, the reason you cannot adequately convey the vision is because it is for an appointed time. Therefore, there is no need for you to go through the anxiety of trying to prove to the world that there is a vision inside of you. As you wait for your promise to be revealed, take comfort in God's perfect timing. Rest assured that, in the fullness of time, your promise *will* speak for itself.

> *Now faith is the substance of things hoped for, the evidence of things not seen* (Hebrews 11:1).

Once the vision or dream has been explained, defined, or revealed, we are overjoyed by the announcement and appearance of the promise as we move closer toward the role of caretaker of our God-given promise. In order to properly nurture this divine destiny, it is important for us to understand that, though the gift is coming through us, it doesn't belong to us. For whatever reason, God has favored and trusted us with the life of His word. It is up to us to adequately prepare for its arrival and facilitate its life on earth.

The Lord has provided the vision. Though we may not be able to explain or articulate in the physical what is being prepared in the spiritual, when the Spirit of God manifests (delivers) your promise in the physical, as mentioned earlier, your promise *will* speak for itself.

> *For now we see through a glass, darkly; but then face to face: now I know in part; but then shall I know even as also I am known* (1 Corinthians 13:12).

Because we are incapable of beholding the end from the beginning, it is important to note that, while we are pregnant with destiny, God will not reveal everything about our destiny from the beginning. As a result, we will experience different stages of preparation designed to draw us into the place where we can ultimately understand the full measure of the weight associated with our purpose.

We must be careful that this partial glimpse into our destiny does not provoke our emotions to produce uncharacteristic and undesirable behavior. For example, excitement about the pregnancy may make it difficult to exercise the discipline necessary for growing our faith. Excitement is good, but being chosen by God to deliver this blessing does not mean that we can afford to slack off in our prayer life, in our praise, or in our giving—that could bring about disastrous results. Allowing excitement to distract us from consistently doing the things that are crucial to the healthy development of our spiritual fetus could not only negatively affect the appropriate growth rate of our promise, but also leave it vulnerable to various spiritual birth defects.

The picture provided by the ultrasound is not meant to become a liability; it is meant to be an asset. For example, if God shows someone that he or she is going to be a doctor, but the person does not apply him or herself in school, then the excitement created from the vision is worthless because the work is not done to bring about the manifestation of that vision. Likewise, our emotional excitement cannot be a substitute for the effort that we should invest as a result of our belief in our promise. James 2:26 states, *"For as the body without the spirit is dead, so faith without works is dead also."* In other words, no work...no wealth...no wonder! If we are not steadfast in our efforts to move forward when the excitement wears off, our faith will dwindle and we will be left weary and wanting! Our belief system will be open to the infections that lurk in everyday life. The realization of our revelation requires an *ultra reliance, extreme belief, and a crazy faith!*

ULTRA, EXTREME, AND CRAZY

In Acts 1, the Word of God reminds us that Jesus instructed His disciples to tarry in the upper room and wait for the promise of the Holy Ghost. It was their *extreme belief* that took them to that secret place after the death, burial, resurrection, and ascension of their beloved Savior. It was their love for their Master, coupled with their extreme belief, that gave them the strength to remain and wait for their promise. The Scripture goes on to say, *"And suddenly there came a sound from heaven as of a rushing mighty wind, and it filled all the house where they were sitting"* (Acts 2:2). They heard an *ultra sound!* Through extreme belief, the disciples received and then gave birth to the presence of the Holy Ghost.

As you may recall, it took ten days for the Holy Ghost to arrive after Jesus ascended into Heaven. Similarly, the full term of a woman's gestation is just over nine months. In other words, the delivery takes place in the beginning of the tenth month. Likewise, your *ultra reliance* on Jesus, your *extreme belief,* and your *crazy faith* will bring about the birth of your destiny. When we are pregnant with destiny and waiting for our promise to be born, there is also a tarrying, or a waiting period. Therefore, while we tarry and wait, even in the midst of seemingly impossible circumstances, our belief must be extreme and our love must be ultra—for it is only in this posture that we will hear the *sound* that produces the image, the vision, the reality of our promise.

This sound called ultra is truly a sound from Heaven! It's a sound generally heard in our prayer closets. Beloved, in order to learn the details pertaining to our fetus of destiny, we need to have an ultrasound. We need to hear from God, for it is not until our beloved Master's sound waves begin to resound within our heart, mind, and spirit that we will ever know what He has called us to do. It is the sound of the Holy Ghost, that mighty rushing wind, that produces the image, the vision, and the reality of our God-ordained destiny.

It should be clearly noted that we do not have the ability to procreate, form, or establish our God-given purpose. Though we may engage in various forms of intimacy, which may result in the releasing or acceptance of seed, by no means can we determine our own destiny. Therefore, it is important for us to understand that what we carry inside us is not the gift we imagined; rather, it is the gift God created. Through the power of the ultrasound, we are able to receive an inside glimpse of the mind of God.

> *Now unto him that is able to do exceeding abundantly above all that we ask or think, according to the power that worketh in us* (Ephesians 3:20).

CHAPTER 9

WATCH YOUR WEIGHT/WAIT

But they that wait upon the LORD shall renew
their strength; they shall mount up with wings
as eagles; they shall run, and not be weary; and
they shall walk, and not faint (Isaiah 40:31).

Let us not become weary in doing good, for
at the proper time we will reap a harvest if
we do not give up (Galatians 6:9 NIV).

Monitoring a pregnant mother's weight is another important aspect of her prenatal care. The data recorded at her initial weigh-in determines how much weight she should gain—or lose—during each trimester and whether she is on track to reach each projected goal. In fact, her doctor may become concerned if she loses weight, doesn't gain enough weight, or gains too much weight.

In addition, her doctor will use the data gathered during subsequent weigh-ins to prescribe a proper diet and exercise regime. Faithfully following these personally tailored instructions increases a mother's chances of remaining on course for a full-term, on-time delivery. Without them, both she and her baby will become susceptible to the often severe or deadly consequences associated with a premature birth or late delivery.

I am excited that the notion of monitoring and controlling weight in the natural has a correlation in the spiritual. It is my hope that, as I share this perspective, you will become excited and motivated to begin a healthy spiritual diet and keep a record of your *wait*. Let's get started.

I have a tendency to monitor my weaknesses. Therefore, the first thing I do every morning and the last thing I do every evening is weigh myself. If I am not in a mode of fasting and praying, what I eat invariably shows up on the scale. Likewise, how much weight one gains during pregnancy is directly connected to what one eats. Because a newborn's weight typically accounts for only twenty-five percent of its mother's total weight gain, her doctor will instruct her to stay far away from foods that are high in fat, sugar, and salt, or that have little or no nutritional value. In addition, she will be cautioned to stay away from foods that have large amounts of preservatives and from substances such as drugs (including several prescribed medications), alcohol, and tobacco. Similarly, it is also important that, while we are pregnant with destiny, we watch what we spiritually consume so that our state of waiting for delivery is not negatively affected by unnecessary burdens, waves of heaviness, lightheadedness, or low energy that would make the process of carrying destiny more difficult or lead to miscarriage.

> **You must continually monitor what you allow into your spirit and how you respond to people and situations.**

For example, from sunup to sundown we must continually monitor what we allow to come into our spirits and how we choose to respond to people and situations. A sharp word to our spouse, a frown to a co-worker, or an impatient tone with our child can cause unnecessary heaviness.

Since excess weight or extreme weight loss can cause severe complications, throughout each day, and especially as we close in prayer at the end of our evening, it is crucial that we ask our Father to lighten our load by forgiving us of our sins and exchanging a spirit of heaviness with a garment of praise.

In addition, we must spend quality time ingesting the Word of God during private reflection and in public worship at our home church. Placing your burdens in God's hands when you are weak and searching for answers in His Word will not only put a healthy amount of meat on your spiritual bones, but it will also allow God to provide His beauty for your ashes. After all, it is far easier to wait for deliverance with the Word on your lips, a song in your heart, and the beauty of His holiness resting upon you.

During this season, it is important that we regularly ingest what I call "home-cooked meals," those prepared especially for us by our spiritual parents (pastors). Since our spiritual parents function as both our primary care physician and obstetrician, they know what we need in our spiritual diet to successfully give birth. In order to sustain the proper level of spiritual nutrition, we must regularly consume the word served by our heavenly Father through the gift of our spiritual fathers or mothers.

A well-balanced, home-cooked meal has several courses—from the singing of the choir, to the preaching of the word, to the witnessing of unsaved souls stepping out of darkness into God's marvelous light. During this season, beloved, let us remember to stay close to home, watch our wait, and not waver from our spiritually prescribed dietary plan. Ensuring the healthy and prosperous delivery of our destiny means avoiding the yoke of heaviness and spiritual malnutrition by faithfully attending church and seeking wisdom and forgiveness through prayer and reading the Word.

The Bible says that "His yoke is easy and His burden is light" (see Matt. 11:30). However, as many of us have experienced, the burden of impatience and the heaviness of self-imposed stress (which the Lord instructs us to cast on Him) can weigh us down to the point that our destiny is either delayed or altogether miscarried. Anxiety married to expectation is one of the worst enemies of divine destiny. We know we are expecting the Lord to do something. That is the basis of our faith. However, we need to rebuke impatience and make every effort to eliminate anxiety so that we can enter into God's rest (see Heb. 4:3). As the Bible states, we must be anxious for nothing, since moving when we are anxious can land us in embarrassing situations (financially, professionally, and in our relationships). We know that God is going to move; we only need to wait on Him and His instructions.

> **Anxiety married to expectation is one of
> the worst enemies of divine destiny.**

MY OWN SEASON OF WAITING

This reminds me of the time when I was waiting for God to release me to pastor. I was preaching in many congregations but not pastoring my own flock. As I sat in various churches throughout my city and state, I knew the anointing and call on my life to pastor was greater than I could ever imagine. When I saw preachers doing very well, I would say to myself, "That is how God is going to bless me." However, the understanding gained by studying the life of Joseph in the book of Genesis allowed me to see that if I shared my vision within my circle of fellow preachers, I would not be well received. So I waited in silence, aware that I wasn't the greatest preacher, yet sure that God would elevate me. I must admit that during this season I became a little anxious.

While waiting to be released to pastor, I was interviewed by a number of churches (one in Roanoke, Virginia, one in Charleston, West Virginia, and one in Montgomery, West Virginia). As I waited to hear back from the churches, I had no idea where the Lord would send me. During that waiting season, I was blessed to become the interim pastor at my father-in-law's church while he recovered from an illness. Soon, I became accustomed to and thoroughly enjoyed preparing sermons, interacting with the congregation before and after service, and ministering to the various needs of the saints. However, once my father-in-law returned to the pulpit, I naturally returned to my seat in the congregation to listen and wait for God to move.

At one point, I entertained a relationship with anxiety. However, I soon realized that if I wanted to see my promise manifested, I needed to divorce anxiety and marry patience. I needed to live in the promise. I needed to settle into the fact that any way and anytime the Lord blessed me, I would be satisfied. Ultimately, I was courted by two churches. One, a very good and stable church with a large congregation, was only fifteen minutes from my home. The other, a much smaller church, was nearly an hour and a half away. Having purposefully divorced anxiety, I honestly did not care where I ended up. My spirit rested in the knowledge that wherever the Lord sent me, I would be satisfied.

Through several church grapevines I learned that both churches were ready to elect their new pastor and that I was the leading candidate in the various unofficial polls of both churches. I remember trying to decide which church I should accept, if both offered me a position. Friends and family urged me to choose the larger church, since it was a more prestigious move. However, I only wanted to follow God's move, so I prayed, "God, I don't know how to do this, but I do know You do. So whichever church calls first is the one I will accept."

During my season of waiting, I continued to minister wherever the Lord directed. One fall day while ministering at the hospital bedside of an old family friend, the telephone rang. The caller, my wife, asked our friend if she could speak with me. I will never forget the love in her voice and the lift of her spirit as she greeted me, "Hello, Pastor!" At first, all I could think was, *Wow,* as the baby leapt within my spirit and confirmed the Lord's assignment.

Content and not the least bit concerned with which church I was called to pastor, after weeks of waiting and years of preparation, my wife informed me that the Lord would have me minister at the smaller church. Though many well-meaning supporters would not understand my acceptance to this seemingly "lesser" call, I was convinced that God had great things for me there.

Size is not an indicator of greatness. In fact, the Lord teaches us to never despise small beginnings; for when we are faithful over a few things, He will make us ruler over many (see Job 8:7; Matt. 25:21). In our youth, we often look for ways that the world can satisfy our physical and spiritual hunger. If we are not careful to seek the Lord's purpose, we will dull our hunger for His presence. While looking for the greatness, take care to remember that with God the lesser can be greater. I am so glad, during that season of destiny, that I was able to wait on the Lord and be of good courage. I am so thankful for the precious fruit of the spirit that I acquired: the invaluable treasure called patience.

Watching your wait, therefore, is critical to obtaining the promise that God has for you. However, you must also pay attention to the extra calories of ambition and to the dangers of adding the extra pounds that come from seeking prominence. I have found that cultivating a spirit of humility concerning the great work that God has placed within you, calls your promise forth and causes your spiritual water to break at its appointed time.

> **Cultivating a spirit of humility causes your spiritual water to break.**

As you can imagine, pregnant women often grow impatient with the pregnancy process. If you have ever been in the company of a pregnant woman, you will observe that she wants to know the gender of her baby. She can't wait! She is tired of carrying the extra pounds. She can't wait! She is ready to give birth. She can't wait! Well, dear saint, if we are pregnant with promise or a seed of destiny, we *have* to wait. We have to wait with the right attitude so that pride, frustration, and impatience don't result in an entire host of related problems.

In Psalm 27:14, the Lord tells us that when we wait on Him and be of good courage, He shall strengthen our hearts. Needless to say, every precaution is taken during a woman's pregnancy to avoid a premature delivery. Full-term babies suffer fewer illnesses because they have had the time to develop the organs and systems that are vital to their health and well-being. Stable breathing and blood pressure are signs that the baby is fully able to function outside the mother's womb.

Developing a consistent spirit of humility and continually striving to perform with excellence at your work, in your ministry, and in your studies, are good indications that your wait, or your patience, is working. You should soon see your destiny grow, flourish, and embody the very promises of God. Romans 1:17 states that *"the just shall live by faith."* In due season, faithfulness, coupled with consistency, will lead to elevation and ever-increasing glory. Isaiah 40:31 reminds us that individuals who wait on the Lord will mount up on wings as eagles. Those who are too anxious for the promise may try to rush the process and ultimately birth what is called an "Ishmael ministry." Remember, Ishmael was the product of impatience.

WAIT, DON'T RUN

In the previous chapter we reviewed how Abram disregarded the God-given instructions designed to give birth to the promised legacy. Sarai's lack of faith led to the burden of confusion, discord, and opposition, rather than divine peace, unity, and affection. Fueled by feelings of inadequacy, Sarai's impatience produced negative thoughts such as, "I can't do this." "I don't have what it takes." "This is hopeless." As is often the case, feelings of inadequacy produces impatience, and impatience produces a future full of opposition, rather than a future full of promise.

Though Sarai could visualize Abram producing the child, she could not envision the promise coming from her own body. She failed to understand that the Lord had connected the promise to both her and Abram. God often uses imperfect people, inferior materials, and impossible circumstances to confound the wise and avoid any confusion as to whom the glory belongs. Weighed down by impatience, Sarai took matters into her own hands and convinced Abram that her servant Hagar's womb would make an excellent substitute for her own.

Abram and Hagar's misguided union produced a seed of opposition that was outside the will of God. Rather than experiencing a much-anticipated sense of relief and joy, everyone involved in the scheme to conceive was distressed by the news of Hagar's pregnancy. Even before the child was born, Hagar adopted an air of superiority toward her mistress, causing Sarai to mistreat her maidservant. Indeed, the atmosphere surrounding the delivery of Hagar's child was wrought with tension. Fleeing Sarai's wrath, Hagar ran to the desert where the angel of the Lord ordered her to return to her oppressor. Before her return, she was instructed to name her son Ishmael, for the Lord had heard her affliction. Then the angel of the Lord proclaimed her son would be a wild man whose hand would be against every man, and to whom every man's hand would be against.

Like Abram and Sarai, many of us get a word from God and *run* with it. However, we must remain patient if we want to avoid producing something that opposes what God has for us. Rushing God's process will cause a self- or man-made gift to be born wild, uncontrollable, confrontational, and more of a heartache than a blessing. Remember, beloved, that *"he which hath begun a good work in you will perform it…"* (Phil. 1:6), and *"Faithful is he that calleth you, who also will do it"* (1 Thess. 5:24).

> **Rushing God's process will cause heartache rather than blessing.**

Inevitably, when we venture off into ungodly territory, before long we come to ourselves and realize that we are not where we are supposed to be. Amazingly, God visits us in our desert place, and, even though we deserve to experience the negative effects of our impatience, He is still willing to guide us out of our misery.

I have been there before. I have jumped out there, on my own, and grabbed something that was at odds with God's plan. A few years back, I received a word from the Lord that I was going to buy a home. All I had to do was wait for Him to bring it to me, but I impatiently decided to find it on my own. Soon, I bought a beautiful brick house with a lush green lawn in a nice neighborhood. As nice as it was, it was not the place where I was purposed to live. Consequently, six months after we moved in, I discovered the house had serious problems.

As I write these words and try to visualize the side of the house where the bedrooms and bathrooms were located, I can only see darkness. In fact, my memories of our days living in that house are cloaked in ominous shadows. I recall that the only serious argument my wife, Martha, and I ever had was in that house, in the master bedroom, in that pool of darkness. If I had just waited for God to bring my promise to me, I could have avoided the headaches and the problems that came along with rushing His plan. A few months after we discovered the problems with the house, the Lord allowed us to move to an even nicer Cape Cod home. It was *wonderful*. In my mind's eye, I can clearly see the entire interior and exterior of that lovely home.

Individuals who rush God's process may think they are getting what He really has for them; however, what they actually end up with is something that is at odds with God's plan. For example, a minister who prematurely starts his ministry because he is opposed to the way his pastor is leading will inevitably bring the same spirit of opposition into his new ministry. In other words, his hand and mouth will be against everyone, and everyone's hand and mouth will be against him. Sadly, this spirit of opposition will define his ministry. Soon his parishioners will not be able to have peaceful, positively productive conversations; rather, they will only have negative things to say, even in regard to the pastor who spiritually birthed them.

> If you rush God's process, you may end up with
> something that is at odds with God's plan.

No doubt Sarai, Abram, and Hagar did not suspect they were sowing a seed that would upset their world as they knew it and produce great suffering and heartache. The first time Hagar left for the desert, she left of her own choice. The next time she left her home, she was forced out. After Isaac (the child of promise) was delivered and established, Ishmael (the child of impatience) jealously mocked God's promise, causing him and his mother to be removed from their home against their wills.

Though it displeased Abram to banish his firstborn son and his mother, he had to do it. Otherwise, the child of promise would not be able to fully mature. Oftentimes, God makes us give up something that we have previously connected ourselves with, in order to connect us to the purpose He has designed especially for us. In other words, if the offspring of impatience still exists, we may very well have to detach (emotionally, mentally, physically, financially, etc.) ourselves from it to avoid the derailment of our divine destiny.

As you continue to read the final pages of this book, remember God has prepared a purpose and place just for you. Yes, beloved, your God-ordained blessings already have your name carved on them. If you are reading this book and have a call on your life to pastor, God already has a flock for you and He *will* lead you to them according to His divine timetable. They may even already be in place, waiting and praying for you to come and shepherd them. I pray that you (pastor or parishioner) remain patient and wait on your ministry.

Let us join together with patience and thanksgiving as we prepare to receive our bundle of joy. Let us listen in expectation for the call of our Lord. Let us prepare our spirits for our *labor praise!*

> *...Eye hath not seen, nor ear heard, neither have entered into the heart of man, the things which God hath prepared for them that love him* (1 Corinthians 2:9).

CHAPTER 10

LABOR PRAISE

*After these things the word of the LORD came unto Abram
in a vision, saying, Fear not, Abram: I am thy shield,
and thy exceeding great reward. And Abram said, LORD
God, what wilt thou give me, seeing I go childless, and
the steward of my house is this Eliezer of Damascus? And
Abram said, Behold, to me thou hast given no seed: and, lo,
one born in my house is mine heir. And, behold, the word
of the LORD came unto him, saying, This shall not be thine
heir; but he that shall come forth out of thine own bowels
shall be thine heir. And he brought him forth abroad,
and said, Look now toward heaven, and tell the stars, if
thou be able to number them: and he said unto him, So
shall thy seed be. And he believed in the LORD; and he
counted it to him for righteousness* (Genesis 15:1-6).

We have been carrying our destiny for nine months. Entering
the tenth month, we must now brace ourselves, for the time of our

delivery is near. Just as labor suddenly comes upon an expectant mother at any hour of the day or night, so our labor will suddenly manifest. Thankfully, God has matured our faith, blessed us with patience, and nurtured us with love. We have looked inside our spiritual wombs, seen the initial image, and received confirmation that we are truly going to give birth. Excitement, anticipation, and even *fear* begin to overwhelm us.

> **God reaches out to soothe you and tell you that you will deliver your promise.**

Doubt that we will be fruitful or able to deliver our destiny is not uncommon. Even Abram, whose name meant "exalted father," suffered from doubt. Yet, as we see in Genesis 15:1-6, God reaches out to us in the midst of our fear and doubt to soothe and inform us that we will certainly deliver our promise.

My goal in this chapter is to help prevent the miscarriage of your destiny during your last trimester. I am confident that God has spoken to you, filled your womb, and formed destiny within your belly. Now that you have made it to this final chapter, let us praise God—for your destiny is about to come forth!

Like an expectant mother, we wonder, *What day and hour will I deliver? Will my baby have ten fingers and ten toes? Where will I be when my water breaks? What is going to happen in the delivery room?* Though questions regarding our destiny and the delivery process abound, do not fear; for Isaiah 66:9 states, *"Shall I bring to the birth, and not cause to bring forth? saith the LORD: shall I cause to bring forth, and shut the womb? saith thy God."* Rest assured, beloved, God *will* bring it to pass! Your blessing is coming out of you! However, like the expectant mother, you will have to go through the labor process in order to *push* it out.

Although conception requires both the mother and the father, only the mother can carry the baby. Therefore, only she can deliver her child through the joys and struggles that come with labor. Likewise, only we, the carriers of our destiny, can birth what is inside us. Thankfully, the Lord will place mature saints (spiritual midwives) and situations in our lives to help us during our time of delivery. As our baby travels head first through the spiritual birth canal and out into the world, our midwives will encourage us to push, and to breathe, and to use the situations that God has given us to safely deliver our promise.

During labor, the most successful delivery techniques help the mother focus on the delivery rather than on the pain. Therefore, expectant mothers are encouraged to take classes designed to familiarize themselves with the labor process. These classes will also let them know what kind of support they can expect from their nurses, midwives, family, and friends.

Early in the labor process, a mother is able to pleasantly interact with people who have little or no knowledge about the different stages of labor or the strategies for coping with the pain of contractions. Once her contractions intensify, irrelevant small talk becomes irritating and turns previously entertaining or educating observers into annoyances rather than soothers of her soul. Therefore, we must intentionally interact with individuals who can prop us up and encourage us to deliver our destiny, such as a spiritual midwife who is able to facilitate, rather than interrupt, the delivery process.

Starting with the initial proclamation from the Lord that we were pregnant with a purpose, God has consistently given us little glimpses of His glory in regard to our future. Each piece of information, each image, each idea that we have received from the Holy Spirit has carried us toward our delivery date. Though there are many areas we still do not understand, we can trust God and rejoice in He who wisely gives us only what we need—and only when we need it. Likewise, we can trust that, as we move closer to our delivery date, God will give us greater clarity.

> **As you move closer to your delivery date,
> God will give you greater clarity.**

Just as He prepared Abram for the delivery of his promise, so God will reveal every detail that you will need to successfully birth your destiny. Although we desire to know every detail, we must focus on our *present* so that we can proceed through the labor process and give birth to what God will give to us in the future. Otherwise, our unbelief and lack of trust in God's word will push the prophecy away.

WAIT ON GOD

Though we cannot know how long we will be in labor or how severe our contractions will be, we cannot let false starts, setbacks, or complications discourage us. We cannot let our desire to know the end before the beginning distract us from our responsibility to seek our daily serving of solace from the daily reading of God's Word. After all, it is our belief in, and our trust of, this daily bread that will give us the strength to push the prophecy forth.

When God tells us He is going to do something and our behavior contradicts His word, we push the prophecy away. We push the words back. We push the blessing back. We push the manifestation back. We push back what God has for us when we do not trust or believe Him. That is what happened to Abram. Because he tried to understand spiritual things with his natural mind, Abram misinterpreted God's promise and mistakenly concluded that Eliezer, his oldest servant, would become his heir rather than his and Sarai's firstborn son.

Perhaps you have heard the Lord's promise that He is going to do great and wonderful things for and through you, but you have not seen it come to pass in *your* presupposed time frame. Perhaps *you've* determined that *you've* walked well enough, and long enough, to know that you are now ready to receive what God has promised. Perhaps in your presupposed conclusion you dare to declare, "Well, God, I'm ready for it!" However, beloved, you can't get "it" until God says you are ready. Only He can judge whether you are ready to receive your promise.

Similarly, a pregnant woman cannot judge *exactly* when she will deliver. She cannot dictate when her water will break, or even where she will give birth. If overly anxious, she can actually begin to falsely sense her body preparing for delivery when, in reality, the baby is not ready to be born. The medical term associated with pre-labor contractions is called Braxton-Hicks. These contractions are considered false because the mother sincerely believes and senses she is in labor, but the baby is not ready to come forth.

Likewise in giving birth to our destiny, we may experience situations that give us a false sense of the beginning stages of labor. If we aren't careful, we can be deceived by spiritual Braxton-Hicks symptoms and believe we are ready to give birth to what God implanted within us. For example, say that we have been waiting for a publisher, investor, husband, or wife, but just when it looks as if the breakthrough we've been waiting for is upon us, the contractions stop (a relationship ends, a partnership dissolves, the deal falls through, etc.). It is quite natural that we considered ourselves ready to welcome our new bundle of joy. However, unless the gift is fully developed within our spiritual womb, our destiny and all who are meant to benefit from it will suffer if it comes forth before its divinely appointed time.

Abram thought he was ready for the birth of his promise. Tired of waiting on God to deliver his promise, Abram came up with his own Plan B. The only way to avoid the unnecessary heartache that comes from impatience is to recognize there is no Plan B with God. If God said it, that's the end of it! God is going to work it out according to His own way, according to His own will, and according to His own time. God will not do it the way you think it should be done. He will not do it when you think it ought to happen. As I said earlier, God will not give your promise to you until you are well prepared.

The normal gestational period for a healthy baby is thirty-eight to forty weeks. Doctors do not want a birth to occur until the baby is prepared to thrive. For example, if a baby is delivered prematurely, its lungs and other organs might not be fully developed. Whether it's a baby or destiny, during the labor and delivery process, we do not have control. We cannot control when our water breaks. We cannot control the contractions. We cannot control when the baby is born. In fact, if we try to rush the process, we may cause our baby, or our destiny, to be deformed by not being obedient throughout the process.

Not only can premature birth affect the baby's survival, it can also catch the parents off guard if they are not prepared for the baby's arrival. God wants the promise to be ready, and He wants you to be prepared to handle it when it arrives. One way to recognize you are ready to receive what God has prepared for you is when you don't lust after it so much that you can't sleep. You will also know you are ready to receive it when you trust God so much that your spirit says, "God *is* the Lord of His Word. He *is* going to do it."

Just as Abram had to wait on God to deliver his promise, so you must also wait on God to deliver the promise He spoke to you. You are only kidding yourself if you think you can do it on your own. In fact, you can't do anything independent of God. You have no power to make the sun come up in the morning or to cause the moon to rise at night. You have no power to make the stars shine, the rain fall, the lightning flash, or the thunder roar. You have no power to wake yourself up in the morning because it is God who touches you with the finger of His love. It is He who causes you to rise from a sleep, which so closely resembles death that it makes people watching you wonder if you might be dead. God has the power to step into the coffin of your sleep, pull you out of that coffin, and tell you to wake up to a brand-new day.

You have no power to stand unless God strengthens the ligaments and the marrow of your bones. You have no power to see until He turns around the upside-down image in your eyes and allows you to focus. It is God who opens your mouth and allows words to form and flow. It is God who causes your lungs to expand and contract and send oxygen throughout your body. It is He who causes your heart to pump blood throughout your body. You can't do that by yourself! That is why you ought to praise Him—He is worthy to be praised! That is why I can't help saying, "If it had not been for the Lord who was on my side, I do not know where I would be!"

PUSH AND PRAISE!

If you've made it this far, you have lived through the devil's attempts to destroy your God-ordained destiny. Now is the time to take the next step into your promised place. Now is the time to birth the love, joy, peace, and prosperity that He has created inside you to bless the world. Now is the time to endure your labor pains with labor praise. Choose to be the example that you were designed to be: a blessing for the entire world to see, so that when people ask you what God has done for you, you can give them your great testimony. You can tell them, "I once was lost, but now I'm found; was blind, but now I see." After all, we were not just created to love God. We have a heavenly obligation to tell everyone we can just how great God really is. We have been created to sing God's praise!

Praise the God who planted the seed of promise within your spiritual womb. Praise Him for the strength He provided over the past few months, or even years, as you diligently carried your promise. You may have experienced the enlarged belly, the swollen feet, the spreading nose, and the sleepless nights—and, now, the time has come! The hour is here! Get ready to deliver the gift! Get ready to deliver the promise! Get ready for the labor praises! Get ready to praise God with all your might!

> **You must praise God through the painful birthing process.**

Just like a woman in labor must experience the pain of her contractions in order to *push* her baby out, you must also go through the pain of labor. Though pain is part of the birthing process, you must praise God through the process. You must praise God for the suffering caused by the pressure of the contractions surrounding your spiritual womb.

You have been carrying this baby for a long time, and now it is time for you to give birth. Now it is time to *push!* Now it is time to *praise!* This is the time to turn over our plates and fast; it is during this critical stage known as labor and delivery. This is not the time to play. This is the time to get down to business. As we turn over our plates, we must shed our inhibitions before the Lord. We must go before Him, naked and unashamed, for it is time to deliver the word that has been growing inside us!

When a mother is in labor, she is not concerned with the way she looks. She is asked to remove all jewelry and articles of clothing. Similarly, when we get ready to bring forth God's gift of life, we need to take off all superficial things that would get in the way of the birthing process, such as pride, doubt, low self-esteem, and our fleshly desires. This is not the time to rely on self or to allow fear or doubt to seize us. Rather, this is the time to completely depend and lean on the Lord.

During this critical season, we must praise God, regardless of our pain and our situations. No matter how we feel, God is ready to cause labor to overtake us. Therefore, we must *push* past how we feel! We must *praise* God! We must *push* past the circumstances of life! We must *praise* God! We must *push* past unhealed hurts, unresolved issues, and unmet needs! We must *praise* God! We must *push* past our quitting point, if we are going to deliver the promise God has set forth in our lives. We must *praise* God because all things work together for good for those who love and believe the Lord! (See Romans 8:28.)

We may appear weak, and the pain of our contractions may tempt us to think we are not strong enough to complete this process. However, we can rely on God's promise that He will not give us more than we can handle (see 1 Cor. 10:13). We can do this. We are fully dilated. Our destiny is crowning. The head is visible! *Push! Push! Push! Praise Him! Praise Him! Praise Him!* We have come too far to turn back now. We have no choice but to bring forth that which God has destined us to deliver. *Push/praise* until it comes! *Push/praise,* we are almost there! *Push! Push! Push! Praise Him! Praise Him! Praise Him!*

Though you may be tempted to dwell on past mistakes or shortcomings, *praise God! Praise Him* with crazy thoughts on your mind, crazy financial deals that went bad, crazy relationships that failed. Regardless of how much it hurts, when it comes time to push, you have to *push/praise. Push/praise* your way into your destiny! *Push/praise* your way into that new career! *Push/praise* your way into your new home! *Push/praise* your way into your new business! *Push/praise* your way into a successful marriage!

As you push/praise, your baby's head will begin to appear with each contraction. When your baby's head remains visible, this is known as crowning. Without a doubt the most painful time of delivery is when the baby's head and shoulders pass through the birth canal. In spite of the pain, there is no turning back. The baby *is* coming. In spite of the painful process, *you will push it out!*

Praise God when you don't feel like it. *Praise God* when you are hurt. *Praise God* when you are confused. *Praise Him* as you push through the pain. *Praise Him* anyhow! *Praise Him* anyway! Sing praises unto the Lord, for He is worthy to be praised! Leap for joy, even though you feel constrained. Shout hallelujah, to push past your pain. Dance before the Lord, naked and unashamed. Wave your hands up in the air; clap them like you just don't care. Praise the King. I promise, you will not regret it. Every time you push, you feel more pain. *Praise God* anyhow! *Praise God* anyway! With every pain, there is a push. With every push, there is a praise. Don't stop praising Him. Magnify Him because your praise will birth your promise. Your promise is coming out of you!

It's here. It's here. Your promise is here!
Hold it. Feel it. Touch it. Smell it.
Kiss the promise of the Risen King.
Behold your destiny.
It is here!

AFTERWORD

By Cornel West

Bishop Glen A. Staples is one of the few great prophetic leaders in contemporary Christendom. He also is my dear brother and fellow freedom fighter in Christ. I was blessed to meet him years ago at Princeton University; I was introduced to him by our beloved sister, Dr. Terri Reid. We break bread together, with his talented son Lamar, on a regular basis. And he is kind to invite me to preach at his historic church, Temple of Praise, every October along with the spiritual genius Bishop T.D. Jakes, comic artist Steve Harvey, and others. This past year, I brought the artistic genius and funkmeister Bootsy Collins and his blessed wife, Patti, to be with us at the church services. His testimony—eloquent and powerful—set the congregation on fire. I shall never forget the deep love, sweet spirit, and holy fire that Sunday at the Temple of Praise. And I can think of no other church in America where we two—Princeton professor and pioneer of funk artistry—could preach and promote the gospel of Jesus Christ. Our sheer appearances and testimonies are grand tributes to the prophetic leadership of Bishop Glen A. Staples.

The grand work and witness of Bishop Staples exemplifies the divine birthing of his promise. This birthing yields a genuine humility in his dealings with others, a profound love in his service to others, and an endless "labor praise" in his authentic devotion to our awesome God. Bishop Staples possesses a unique self-confidence and earned self-respect that enables him to move smoothly from prince to pauper, White House to crack house, CEO to everyday Daddy-o. His divinely ordained spiritual calling reminds me of his inimitable mentor, Bishop T.D. Jakes. His divinely infused personal style reminds me of the gentle genius, Curtis Mayfield. And Bishop Staples' own distinctive genius reminds me of what Jesus Christ can do when we prevent the miscarriage of destiny by surrendering our lives to God and becoming vessels for divine birthing. Bishop Staples has enriched my life. Let this book and his ministry enrich your life, too!

ABOUT
BISHOP GLEN A. STAPLES

Bishop Glen A. Staples, known around the world for his oratorical gifting and anointed ability to teach the Word of God, serves as the senior pastor of the 14,000-member Temple of Praise International located in Washington, D.C. Bishop Staples also serves as the presiding prelate of the Temple of Praise International Fellowship of Churches, overseeing more than 350 churches worldwide.

IN THE RIGHT HANDS, THIS BOOK WILL CHANGE LIVES!

Most of the people who need this message will not be looking for this book. To change their lives, you need to put a copy of this book in their hands.

> *But others (seeds) fell into good ground, and brought forth fruit, some a hundred-fold, some sixty-fold, some thirty-fold* (Matthew 13:8).

Our ministry is constantly seeking methods to find the good ground, the people who need this anointed message to change their lives. Will you help us reach these people?

> *Remember this—a farmer who plants only a few seeds will get a small crop. But the one who plants generously will get a generous crop* (2 Corinthians 9:6).

EXTEND THIS MINISTRY BY SOWING
3 BOOKS, 5 BOOKS, 10 BOOKS, OR MORE TODAY,
AND BECOME A LIFE CHANGER!

Thank you,

Don Nori Sr., Founder
Destiny Image
Since 1982

DESTINY IMAGE PUBLISHERS, INC.

"Promoting Inspired Lives."

VISIT OUR NEW SITE HOME AT
WWW.DESTINYIMAGE.COM

FREE SUBSCRIPTION TO DI NEWSLETTER

Receive free unpublished articles by top DI authors, exclusive discounts, and free downloads from our best and newest books.
Visit www.destinyimage.com to subscribe.

Write to: Destiny Image
              P.O. Box 310
              Shippensburg, PA 17257-0310

Call: 1-800-722-6774

Email: orders@destinyimage.com

For a complete list of our titles or to place an order
online, visit www.destinyimage.com.

FIND US ON FACEBOOK OR FOLLOW US ON TWITTER.

www.facebook.com/destinyimage   facebook
www.twitter.com/destinyimage   twitter